THE
EFFICIENCY
OF
CAPITALISM

Copyright©2019 by Germinal G. Van
All Rights Reserved
Book written by Germinal G. Van
Cover designed by Germinal G. Van
Published by Germinal G. Van and Kindle Direct Publishing
authorgerminalgvan@gmail.com
ISBN: 978-1792604492
Printed in the United States

4

Germinal G. Van

Author of *Reflection On Identity Politics*

THE EFFICIENCY OF CAPITALISM

*The Economic and Political Philosophy
of the Free-Market*

Kindle Direct Publishing

6

TABLE OF CONTENTS

References
171

10

ABOUT THE AUTHOR

_____

Germinal G. Van is an author, political essayist, and libertarian writer. He is a member of the Libertarian Party of Chicago, a member of the Midwest Political Science Association, and the Communication Director of Joshua Flynn, political candidate for Illinois State Legislature for the general election of 2020.

His writings focus on the subjects of political philosophy, constitutional politics, political economy, and social theory. He holds a bachelor's degree in political science at the Catholic University of America and a master's degree in political management from the George Washington University.

Mr. Van is originally from the Republic of Côte d'Ivoire and now lives in Chicago, Illinois. He has become an author since 2018 and has published four books since. He has also published several articles with the *Foundation for Economic Education* and the *Libertarian Institute*.

Books published by the same Author

American Political Culture: An Observation From The Outside

Equal Under The Law: Reflection on Amendment XIV and the Concept of Citizenship

Essays On Issues: The Fundamentals of American Politics

Reflection On Identity Politics: Here Is Why Identity Politics Divides More Than It Unites

14

ACKNOWLEDGEMENTS

As usual, my wife and my sister come first in the list of people that are being acknowledged following the fulfillment of the manuscript. My wife and my sister have had dearly contribute to the production of each of my books through their relentless support. Without their support I would not be able to produce such works.

Secondly, I would like to thank my friend, John P. Fahy for always bringing his intellectual perspicacity into my writings. John is the Democratic Committeeman of Warren township, New Jersey. He has been a pioneer in his community and has largely contributed to the advancement of local politics in New Jersey.

Lastly, I'd like to thank my childhood friend Stan McWest for his critical insight within my work. His sharp insights have enabled me to ameliorate my writing and argumentative skills. Stan is an International Project Coordinator at the Education Development Center (EDC).

FOREWORD

The development of economic and political thought has undergone a series of shifts and transformations since late antiquity. Aristotle was one of the first to write about exchange value versus use-value. Centuries after this the world experienced the rise and fall of the Roman Empire. The fall, which a multitude of economists and historians now attribute to failed economic and monetary policy. When Europe rose out of the Dark Ages, new groups and writers began to ponder the reasons for economic success and failure among societies. Adam Smith laid the foundation with his seminal work *The Wealth of Nations*, where he attempted to explain in a logical fashion the reasons for the apparent successes of capitalist and mercantilist economies. After Smith's death, his own country entered a new era with the beginning of the Industrial Revolution. England experience a huge surge in the growth of steam mills, which began popping up across the country, especially in cities like Manchester and Leeds. A young man named Friedrich Engels, who was an heir to some of these mills, witnessed firsthand the lives and the struggles of the factory workers, inspiring him to write his now famous text *The Condition of the Working Class in England.*

While Capitalism brought about great success, development, and innovation, there still seemed to be a large group of people excluded from this success. Karl Marx was one of the first people who began working on a systematic analysis of capitalism. He saw is as a stage of history, the successor of the feudal age and system that had collapsed before it. He predicted that Capitalism would eventually collapse, just like Feudalism did. We know now that Capitalism has proven to be much more resilient than Marx had imagined.

Since Marx's time, there have arisen many different ways and schools of thought aimed at analyzing our current economic system and what actions, if any, should be taken by world governments. The Austrian School states that we essentially have the best capitalist economic system when it is free from government influence and interference. This lies in stark contrast to the Keynesian School of economics thought, which rose out of the work of British Economist, John Maynard Keynes, that asserts macroeconomic stabilization by governments and central banks via fiscal and monetary policies can lead to a more efficient economic system.

Germinal Van plants himself firmly in the Austrian School, but whether someone approaches economics from a left-wing or right-wing perspective, Van's analysis still presents a refreshing and novel take on our current economic system. The reader will certainly enjoy and appreciate this text and the many more works of Van which are certain to follow it.

John Patrick Fahy
Member of the Watchung Hills Regional High School Board of Education and the Somerset County Democratic Committee.

PREFACE

Capitalism, as I have numerously said, is the greatest economic system ever created by human beings. It is the only economic system that has enabled the creation of wealth. As I have lived in the United States for nine years, I noticed how many people living in America, have cultivated a sentiment of anger, jealousy, and resentment against capitalism. People see capitalism as the evil system that incentivizes more inequality. They see capitalism as the system that makes the rich richer and the poor poorer. This is the message that Karl Marx and all the people who have adhered to his resentful philosophy, have conveyed throughout the world for two centuries. Today, the American people also believe in that erroneous premise. Evidence have demonstrated that socialism is the economic system and political ideology that makes the poor poorer. The Soviet Union is a prominent example of the failure of socialism. A two-third of the Soviet population was extremely impoverished and lagged economically while the remaining one-third was wealthy because it was part of the Politburo.

Centrally-planned economy created more inequalities. Capitalism has lifted billions of people out of poverty. Tremendous economic progress has been made since the fall of the Berlin Wall in 1989 and the dissolution of the Soviet Union in 1991. According to an article published on the British magazine *The Economist;* between 1990 and 2010, the number of people living in extreme poverty has significantly fallen from 43 percent to 21 percent, which is a reduction of almost 1 billion people.[1] Without capitalism and the implementation of a free-market economy, these results would have not been possible.

Capitalism is a system that does unequally redistribute the wealth; nonetheless, it is the system that abundantly rewards those who produce capital and create wealth. Capitalism is the system that gives the possibility to individuals to become billionaires. It is not a coincidence if individuals like Warren Buffet or Jeff Bezos are today the wealthiest people on the planet. They are the ones who create wealth, employment, and capital. They are the ones that innovate and stimulate the economy. Capitalism make the rich richer and the poor richer. It is a win-win, a system of mutual benefits.

---

[1] Edtiors, "Towards the End of Poverty," *The Economist*. (2013).
https://www.economist.com/leaders/2013/06/01/towards-the-end-of-poverty. Article. Web.

I chose to write this book because I believe that it is quintessentially imperative to remind people that whether they like it or not, whether they want to be ungrateful about it or not, capitalism is the only system that has improved the lives of billions of people and the system that has advanced the human condition for the better. My goal is to fully explicate why capitalism is still the greatest system despite all the critics that have attempted to say otherwise.

INTRODUCTION

———————

Capitalism is an economic and political system in which a country's trade and industry are controlled by private owners for profit rather than by the state. The substance of capitalism emphasizes on the premise that the means of production are concentrated in the hands of individuals rather than the state. In a capitalistic system, the individual owns his labor. It suggests that an individual owns what he produces.

Capitalistic ownership means two things— first the owners control the factors of production.[2] Second, they drive their income from

———————

[2] Amadeo, Kimberly, *Capitalism, Its Characteristics, with Pros and Cons*, The Balance, Economic Models, Economic Theory,

their ownership—that gives them the ability to operate their companies efficiently.[3] It also provides them with the incentive to maximize profit.[4] Capitalism requires a free-market economy to succeed.[5] It distributes goods and services according to the laws of supply and demand.[6] The law of demand articulates that when demand increases for a particular product; prices rise when competitors realize they can make a higher profit, they increase production. The greater supply reduces prices to a level where only the best competitors remain.[7]

The greatest factor of capitalism is the free-market. Capitalism cannot function without a free-market economy. Free-market is simply the economic organization in which prices are

---

December 29, 2018, https://www.thebalance.com/capitalism-characteristics-examples-pros-cons-3305588. Article. Web.
[3] Amadeo, Ibid.
[4] Amadeo, Ibid.
[5] Amadeo, Ibid.
[6] Amadeo, Ibid.
[7] Amadeo. Ibid.

determined by unrestricted competition between privately owned businesses. Free-market economy is the main engine of capitalism because it is the system whereby voluntary exchanges take place between individuals. As these voluntary exchanges take place, both parties involved in the exchange benefit from each other. The opponents of capitalism argue that the free-market economy is an individualistic, egotistical, and immoral system because it generates a great gap of economic and social inequality between members of society. They blame the free-market economy for stimulating income inequality between individuals and maintain that income inequality increases the level of poverty. Moreover, they argue that the intervention of the state is necessary in the distribution of wealth; that it reduces income inequality and diminishes the inequality gap between social classes. First and foremost, the free-market economy is, of course, an individualistic system. It is a legitimate individualistic economic system. And it is quite normal to be an individualistic economic system because the individual is the main actor, the principal factor of the means of production. Adjunctively, the free-market economy is an ultimately moralistic system because the individual is rewarded for the production of his labor.

In the Old Testament of the *Holy Bible*, in chapter 3 verse 19 of the Genesis, it is said "It is by the sweat of your face that you will eat bread, until you return to the earth from which you were taken; for you are dust, and you will return to the dust."[8] This powerful biblical phrase elaborates the nature of capitalism. It accentuates on the precept that there are no rewards without effort. This effort entails hard work, dedication, and determination. Similarly, capitalism shows that the accumulation of an individual's wealth is based on the work and the considerable amount of effort that he has invested to obtain concrete

---

[8] Genesis, Chapter 3, Versed 19, The Old Testament, The Holy Bible.

outcomes. In other words, free-market capitalism is legitimately a moral system because it enhances human value and fairness.

"Take it from the rich and give it to the poor is the solidest way to ensure justice and social equality." This is the new precept taught to the youth of this first quarter of the 21st century. Today, to say that you are for capitalism, free-market, free and voluntary exchange of goods and services, profit, and wealth; is to say that you support greed, selfishness, and evil. High School and college students are all indoctrinated by cultural Marxism. They are taught today that, to be considered by society as a good human being, you must believe in equality, you must believe that the state holds your future and that the government is your salvation. They are taught that it is okay if the government raises taxes, and arbitrarily deprives you of your liberty and property. They are taught that it is okay if the government does so, and you should not complain about it because it is done so to ensure equality;

and to guarantee equality, the state has to do dirty things sometimes. Yet capitalism, the system that the youth has been taught to hate, is the best economic system that could ever exist in human recorded history.

College professors and modern intellectuals do not teach students that capitalism is the most compatible system with human nature. College professors and modern intellectuals do not teach students that human beings are naturally individualistic beings because the highest moral purpose of a human being is the freedom to pursue his own self-interests. College professors and modern intellectuals do not teach students that "profit" is a natural element of the human condition because human beings are naturally inclined to keep the profit of what they produce. College professors and modern intellectuals do not teach students that private ownership is what maintains the self-preservation of a human being. College professors and modern intellectuals do not teach students that the human condition started in poverty and that the use of skills, talents, and abilities are what generate the utility of scarce resources, the creation of wealth, and the production of capital. College professors and modern intellectuals do not teach students that "no one will take better care of your property than yourself." College professors and modern intellectuals do not teach students that government always mismanage resources because it prevents the market to allocate them. College professors and modern intellectuals do not teach students that government intervention stimulates more inequalities although it has been substantiated. College professors and modern intellectuals do not teach students that laissez-faire capitalism is the only system in which human beings can truly maximize their potential to elevate themselves to better ends. No! Instead, they teach them that "whatever you earn, you don't deserve it." They teach them that "whatever you possess is not yours because you didn't build it; someone else built that for you." They teach them that natural inequality is a curse and that conformity is better for all of us in order to be equal. The generations to come are being indoctrinated by an elite that does not care about them. If we do not teach them the value of classical liberalism again, we will surely regret it for a very long time.

Lastly, social inequality is natural, and capitalism did not create social inequality. People are more focused on redistributing the wealth rather than concentrating on what produces the wealth. They perceive poverty as a curse or something abnormal, whereas the human race was initially designed in poverty. The first humans were not born rich or wealthy. They created wealth by hunting and commercializing the product that they have hunted. They established trade-offs among themselves in which each of them made profit from these trade-offs. As the trade-offs substantially grew, they established a market wherein prices could be determined based on the demand. This is how wealth started within the human race. That is to say, everybody started in poverty. Social inequality became a casual factor of the human condition when the first humans who created wealth passed it along to their heirs, and their heirs kept accumulating more goods and possessions to amplify the wealth that they have inherited.

The objective of this book is to promulgate the apology for capitalism. Apology; not in the sense of presenting excuses for capitalism's imperfections, but an apology in the sense of asserting a defense, like the way Socrates defended himself before the Athenian council prior to his execution. Therefore, this book is a defense of capitalism. A justification for its legitimacy and for its necessity. The central idea is to show that, despite its flaws, capitalism has always proved to be a system in which individuals are economically better off when they contribute to the production of wealth by mutual and voluntary exchange of goods and services. The manuscript is subsequently divided into two major parts. The first part examines the economic philosophy of the free- market. It investigates the factors that make capitalism an efficient and sustainable economic system. The second part elaborates on the political philosophy of the free-market. It examines and expounds the components that advance the principles of capitalism as an effective system.

PART I

THE ECONOMIC
PHILOSOPHY
OF
THE FREE-MARKET

Chapter 1

THE DIVISION OF LABOR

As the doctrine of the separation of powers in politics focuses on the principle that each branch of government acts independently from one another with the goal of conveying government action; similarly, the division of labor is a doctrine in economics which stresses the assignment of different parts of a manufacturing process or tasks to different people in order to improve efficiency. It is the system of a work process into a number of tasks, with each task performed by a separate person or group of persons.[9] This concept became a well-known and prominent doctrine in political economy when Adam Smith published in 1776 his greatest work entitled *An Inquiry Into The Nature and Causes of The Wealth of Nations* also known for the short appellation as *The Wealth of Nations*. In *The Wealth of Nations*, Adam Smith argued that the division of labor enables each individual to focus on a given task and to acquire a specialization within that task. Its importance in economics lies in the fact that a given number of workers can produce far more output using the division of labor compared to the same number of workers each working alone.[10] The noteworthy point about the doctrine of the division of labor is that it;

---

[9] Editors of Encyclopedia Britannica, "Division of Labour", *Encyclopedia Britannica,* https://www.britannica.com/topic/division-of-labour. Article History.

[10] Munger, Michael, "Division of Labor", *The Library of Economics and Liberty (2017),* https://www.econlib.org/library/Enc/DivisionofLabor.html . Article. Web.

except for the fact that it increases the productivity of the labor; also increases the stimulation of wealth.

Adam Smith furthered his theory of the division of labor as he stressed that labor is divided into the number of operations that fit the extent of market.[11] For example, in a smaller market, perhaps three workers, each performing several operations, could be employed—in a city or small country, 18 workers might be employed—in an international market, the optimal number of workers would be even larger.[12] Furthermore, Smith elaborates on the fact that a decentralized market exchange fosters the division of labor because the productive capacities are learned. As a matter of fact, when an individual solely focuses on the task he has been assigned to, he subsequently begins to develop a skill related to that task. And the maximization on that skill generates profits once the mechanism of that task

---

[11] Munger, *Ibid.*
[12] Munger, *Ibid.*

is utterly mastered. As Bruce Lee once famously said: "I fear not the man who practiced ten thousand kicks once, but I fear the man who has practiced one kick ten thousand times."[13] This proverb of the famous Chinese American actor and philosopher substantiates explicitly that an individual who has capitalized or optimized on one single skill is literally unbeatable in that specific realm because he knows and masters with diligence, the procedure and mechanism of this specific task in which he has developed his ability to perform in that realm. The maximization of skills increases and promotes, certainty or, I would say, the likelihood that the operation of the task will generate profit. Let's use a hypothetical scenario. For example, let's suppose that Mr. W, an individual who works for XYZ Company, which is a pencil manufacturing company, has developed the ability to transform simple pieces of wood into pencils. Within the

---

[13] Bruce Lee Quote.

three years of working for XYZ Company, Mr. W's entire job was to use a very specific machine with quite a complex mechanism to transform pieces of wood into pencils. The mechanism consisted of cutting the wood into the shape of a pencil then inserting a pencil lead into the wood once that wood has been cut. For three years, Mr. W has only been doing that. Nothing else. It became a routine for him because he has capitalized upon that skill he developed. Thereafter three years working for that company, Mr. W has decided to leave the company and to open his own pencil business. He saved enough money to buy the exact machinery that he was using at XYZ. Moreover, the new business that he administers, uses the same tools to produce pencils as XYZ Company does, and his business sells these pencils at a cheaper price than XYZ. When Mr. W opened his pencil business, his clientele was relatively low. He had per day ten requests for pencil-making. The clientele was significantly satisfied with the production of pencils that his business has been providing. Nine months later, the demand for pencil-making has tripled and the business income has substantially augmented. The fact that Mr. W knew how to produce pencils thanks to the expertise he has acquired in this domain, makes him an asset and a reliable product-maker for pencil users, and also a serious contender for XYZ Company. This example illustrates how the specialization of one task by an individual strengthens the skills of the worker and incentivizes wealth.

The division of labor is surely the pillar for an effective free-market economic system. As Adam Smith asserted, the division of labor reduces every man's business to some one simple operation, and by this operation the sole employment of his life, necessarily increases very much the dexterity of the workman.[14] It is a humongous waste of time to attempt learning

---

[14] "Division of Labor (Adam Smith)", *General Principles of Management,* https://ozgurzan.com/management/management-theories/adam-smith/. Article. Web.

different skills on different operations instead of investing that same time in optimizing that one skill that one already knows. Since the laborers did not have to focus on multiple jobs, this saved them precious time.[15] It was an important benefit that led to increase production and stimulate wealth.[16] Productive labor could create surplus value which could again be invested in production.[17] The fundamental component of the division of labor is efficiency. As Adam Smith explained in the first chapter of *The Wealth of Nations* entitled "Of The Division of Labor," in a metallurgy company, one worker is responsible for ensuring that the iron is ready for forging, another worker oversees the medal, another worker focuses on straightening the iron, and another worker cuts it and so on until the nail

---

[15] Pratap, Abhijeet, "Division of Labor: Adam Smith", *Cheshnotes,* October 1st, 2016, updated in September 28, 2018. https://www.cheshnotes.com/2016/10/division-labor-adam-smith/. Article. Web.
[16] Pratap, *Ibid.*
[17] Pratap, *Ibid.*

becomes a finished product.[18] This breakdown in production allows workers to only focus on a small part of the fabrication of a commodity.[19] The focus on each part of the commodity engenders efficiency. Efficiency is the most fundamental element of productivity in a laissez-faire economy. The laissez-faire economy incentivized efficiency in the production of commodity because the production itself is made by human action.

The division of labor is the fundamental and foundational element of a free-market economy and of capitalism in general. Indeed, the greatness of capitalism rests on the efficiency of the production of labor. The production of labor is maintained and promulgated by human action. The specialization of a skill in a particular field or realm allows the workers to become an expert,

---

[18] Reyes, Raul, "An Inquiry Into The Division of Labor" (2013). *University Honors Theses.* Paper 27. https://pdxscholar.library.pdx.edu/cgi/viewcontent.cgi?article=1024&context=honorstheses.

[19] Reyes, *Ibid.*

asset for himself and for the firm in the labor market and also for the global economy.

Chapter 2

THE CREATION OF WEALTH

The creation of wealth occurs only through the course of human action. It implies that the production of labor asymmetrically produces wealth. The production of wealth is ingrained in individual achievements. To produce wealth, an individual needs talent, skills, ability, drive, determination, discipline and also a little bit of luck. Individual achievements are an essential factor of the stimulation and accumulation of wealth because the essence of wealth lies in human capital and human capital enforces the production of labor powers.

The United States is the wealthiest nation on earth because it had or use to have a laissez-faire economic system in which individuals are free to pursue their economic incentives as they maximize their skills. The abundant accumulation of wealth in the United States is the result of the production of labor invigorated by human action, which means individual effort, and personal performance. Undeniably, the United States is the only country where one will find multi-millionaires on a regular basis, and billionaires abundantly. It is important to understand that the United States is not a country founded on aristocratic rule or by a bourgeois order. In Europe, however, most European societies have been constructed on social classes. It was built upon classes in which individuals did not truly have to stimulate wealth on their own merit since they belonged to an aristocratic family. Nonetheless, it does not mean that there were not some individuals who did not make it to the top as they started from scratch. It, of course, exists but it is more of a rareness than a common societal norm like in the United States.

A wealthy English individual, living in England for example, did not necessarily create the wealth he possesses on his own. He generally comes from a wealthy family that belongs to the British aristocratic class. Thus, this wealthy English individual has inherited the family's wealth to increase his own wealth, whether that wealth he has inherited is a real estate, a business, or a huge sum of money bequeathed by his father. Therefore, he did not create the wealth he possesses because he is not the fundamental source that has stimulated and generated that wealth. Most wealthy Europeans have inherited the wealth they possess rather than creating it on their own since they originated from a social class that has already created that wealth. That is why the stimulation of wealth in Europe is strongly resented compare to that of the United States. That is why the redistribution of wealth in Europe is strongly regulated by government unlike in the

United States. Proletarians and middle-class Europeans staunchly abhor aristocratic Europeans because they argue that bourgeois Europeans exploit their labor to make accumulate wealth. A wealth that they do not deserve.

On the other side of the Atlantic, the social phenomenon that leads to the creation of wealth is the credo of American culture. The fundamental character of American culture is based on economic liberty with an emphasis on the freedom of the individual. By asserting the word "individual", I imply human action separately performed by individuals in the productivity of societal advancement. The quintessential element of American individualism is rooted in the precept of the creation of wealth and the quest for freedom. And the individual is the main commensurable unit of these two principles. Regarding the creation of wealth, the substantial difference between the United States and European capitalist countries lies in the access to economic opportunities, resources and human capital. In fact, the United States is not a society founded on social classes like in Europe. Any individual residing in the United States has access to the opportunities, resources and human capital to become at least economically self-sufficient. The access to opportunity in Europe is a scarcity. For example, if we look at the case of Europe, it is extremely difficult, or even impossible for an African individual to leave his family and all his possessions in his homeland, immigrate to Europe and suddenly become rich regardless of the effort he has invigorated to create wealth. Unless that African individual is an athlete, it is almost impossible for him to become as wealthy as he wished to be in Europe. Many Africans immigrate to Europe for educational purposes and financial security. Some of them even have the highest educational attainment in a given European society. Nonetheless, these same highly educated Africans do not earn as much as they should despite their educational achievements because certain exogeneous factors such race or culture impede their ascension within European society. But let's say that very same African individual who is moving to the United States, does have, indeed, broader opportunities to create wealth for him (and maybe for his family) if he puts the effort required and necessary to generate that wealth. African immigrants in the United States have one of the highest percentages of educational attainment.[20] This result shows the output that African immigrants produce in order to incentivize the American economy. Individuals in the United States become extremely wealthy because the free-market economy that we have, does fully reward individual achievement since the individual itself is the commensurable unit of the production of wealth. It entails that for an

---

[20] Simmons, Ann, "African immigrants are more educated than most—including people born in U.S." *Los Angeles Times*. January 12, 2018. https://www.latimes.com/world/africa/la-fg-global-african-immigrants-explainer-20180112-story.html. Article. Web.

individual to accumulate more wealth, he must go beyond, way beyond his limits. The excess of individual action in favor of the production of labor amplifies the accumulation of wealth. An individual who owns more than three businesses inevitably becomes a wealthy person because each of his businesses earn him profit and consequently expands his net worth. In American, an immigrant can easily own more than two businesses. In Europe, however, this boon is significantly restricted. Immigrants in Europe generally speaking, have a hard time thriving economically because European governments make economic opportunities a scarcity to them. As I foresaid, America is the only country in the world where an individual, starting from nothing, can become a millionaire, or even a billionaire if that person pursues her economic interests wherein individual action deliver great outputs. I will illustrate three examples to support my argument. These three examples are Oprah

Winfrey, Arnold Schwarzenegger, and Bill Clinton.

The main factor that binds these three individuals is the fact that they are all self-made individuals. Today, Oprah Winfrey is unequivocally the wealthiest black woman in America. Her net worth is around $ 2.8 billion as of 2018.[21] She came from a very modest family. She started off as a television reporter in Nashville, Tennessee in the 1970s before being offered her own 30-minute talk show on WLS-TV, Chicago's ABC affiliate station.[22] In 1986, it was expanded to an hour and renamed the Oprah Winfrey Show.[23] It became the highest-rated American talk show ever, running for 25 years—from 1986 to 2011. After it became nationally syndicated, Winfrey became a millionaire at just

---

[21] Langone, Alix, "Oprah Winfrey Is Worth Nearly $3 Billion. Here's How She Made Her Money". *Time*, March 9, 2018, http://time.com/money/5092809/oprah-winfrey-net-worth-billionaire/. Article. Web.
[22] Langone, Ibid.
[23] Langone, Ibid.

thirty-two years old.[24] Oprah launched *O, The Oprah Magazine* in 2000 while she was still running the Oprah Winfrey Show.[25] Over the last 15 years, the publication has brought in $1 billion in consumer revenue, according to Women's Wear Daily.[26] Oprah continued expanding on her success in the media world, wiring numerous best-selling books and acting in and producing critically acclaimed films.[27] She subsequently started the OWN: The Oprah Winfrey Network, a woman-centric cable network.[28] She sold a 24.5% stake in OWN for $70 million to Discovery Communications, which now controls 75 % of the company.[29] The success of Oprah is clearly not a random fact of nature. It is a succession of events grounded in hard work and individual action. The second example of individual achievements is

---

[24] Langone, Ibid.
[25] Langone, Ibid.
[26] Langone, Ibid.
[27] Langone, Ibid.
[28] Langone, Ibid.
[29] Langone, Ibid.

Arnold Schwarzenegger. The reason why I chose Arnold Schwarzenegger is because he is a foreigner like myself, who came to the United States with nothing but his dreams, and successfully fulfilled the American Dream. Arnold Schwarzenegger is famously known to be a bodybuilder, an actor, and a politician. He was even Governor of the State of California from 2003 to 2011. Arnold Schwarzenegger immigrated to the United States from Austria in 1968. Before moving to the United States, Arnold Schwarzenegger was constantly going to the gym. His goal was to one day becoming the greatest bodybuilder in the world. His ambition and determination enabled him to win at eighteen years of age, the Junior Mr. Europe Contest.[30] The fact that Schwarzenegger won the European bodybuilding contest, demonstrates that he developed a skill in bodybuilding. It was a skill

---

[30] Shull, Ed, "How Arnold Became Rich", *Filthy Lucre*, August 8, 2018. https://filthylucre.com/how-arnold-schwarzenegger-became-rich/. Article. Web.

that he maximized upon to make profit. This early success paved the way for his greatest achievement in bodybuilding. As he understood that concept, he subsequently moved to America with that same mindset of furthering the maximization of his skills in the realm of bodybuilding. A year after his settlement in the United States in 1969, Arnold Schwarzenegger competed in the Mr. Olympia Bodybuilding Contest. His attempt was a failure. The subsequent year, in 1970, he won the competition, which made him the youngest Mr. Olympia at the age of twenty-three. Schwarzenegger won the competition six consecutive times, which significantly expanded his accumulation of wealth. Of course, he gained world fame as a movie actor, then became involved in politics, but the true source of the production of his wealth was in the skills he has maximized to become the greatest bodybuilder of all time. The third example to support my argument is the 42nd President of the United States, William Jefferson

Clinton. Although I politically disagree with President Clinton, it worth mentioning him as a self-made man who also completed the American Dream through hard work. Bill Clinton comes from a working-class family. His father died when he was a baby and his mother, Virginia Blythe, was a nurse who remarried to Roger Clinton, Sr. who was a car salesman. Bill Clinton attended Georgetown University for his undergraduate career under a full scholarship because his parents could not afford college tuitions. The two greatest skills of Bill Clinton have been his charisma and his intellectual versatility. He has maximized on his charisma to extend his skill of persuasion. He had the ability to shape and manipulate human emotions. As a politician, it is a fundamental skill necessary to attract voters and keep control over the audience. He has also capitalized on his intellectual abilities to strengthen his argumentative skills. Bill Clinton understood that he could make profit in politics as long as his charisma and persuasive skills would take him to the pinnacles of power. As a Georgetown student, he was elected president of the student council for student government. He subsequently went on to Yale Law School to pursue a law degree; still under full scholarship. His intellectual proficiencies enabled him to obtain good grades which qualified him for the obtainment of selective scholarships. His very first salary was as an assistant professor of law at the University of Arkansas. Bill Clinton accumulated wealth in state politics when he was Governor of the State Arkansas. That wealth allowed him to meet the financial eligibility to run for President. The wealth of Bill Clinton substantially expanded after his presidency.

The main purpose of using these three individuals was to spotlight the fact that they all start with absolutely nothing and made it to the top by successively creating wealth through individual action that incentivized the production of labor and through the efficiency of the maximization of skills. If it was in Europe, these three individuals (especially Oprah Winfrey) would not have been as wealthy and prosperous. The capitalist society we have in the United States heavily rewards human productivity, and those who go beyond their full potential. Individual achievements are indeed, the most significant factor for the creation of wealth because it empowers human capital. Individual achievements encapsulate four main elements that vitalize its legitimacy and essence. These factors are entrepreneurship, personal responsibility, competition and family values.

First, let's examine the first factor of individual achievements, which is entrepreneurship. According to *Investopedia*, which is a very credible source to search for definitions and meanings; an entrepreneur is an individual who rather than working as an employee founds and runs a small business, assuming all the risks and rewards of the venture.[31] Entrepreneurs play a key role in any economy.[32] These are the people who have the power, skills and initiative necessary to anticipate current and future needs and bring new good ideas to the market.[33] The main characteristic of entrepreneurship is unequivocally innovation. As a practical matter, entrepreneurs are the innovators of the economy.[34] Entrepreneurs are those who have the ability to shape the market economy by invigorating a new product or initiating a solution to a service. Innovation is the element that encourages new endeavors. As an individual capitalizes on his skills, he begins to concurrently innovate new ideas and new plans to make profit from that skill he has been developing.

---

[31] Kenton, Will, "Entrepreneur", *Investopedia*, March 20, 2018, Article.
[32] Kenton, Ibid.
[33] Kenton, Ibid.
[34] Shukla, Amitabh, "The Importance of Innovation in Entrepreneurship", *Paggu*, 2017, https://www.paggu.com/entrepreneurship/the-importance-of-innovation-in-entrepreneurship/. Article. Web.

Entrepreneurship cannot work in an economy which is strongly regulated by the state because the state will impose a set of regulations that would significantly reduce competition and incentives. Economic growth occurs when the market is, at least, reasonably deregulated, and when the quality of service or the new products on the market, satisfies the needs of the consumer. For this phenomenon to happen, innovation must be at the epicenter of the process. An easy example of product innovation could be the launching of touch screen cell phones when the world was still using a keypad on cell phones.[35] Process innovation can be seen in capital-intensive industries that have to replace manual labor with machines, therefore, increasing their production and reducing their

---

[35] "Concepts and Characteristic of Entrepreneurship" *Entrepreneurship Development,* https://www.toppr.com/guides/business-studies/entrepreneurship-development/concepts-and-characteristics-of-entrepreneurship/. Article. Web.

costs.[36] Another type of innovation can be the one concerned with usage.[37] For example, cell phones are now used for various functions other than just making phone calls and sending text messages; creating and editing various files and documents, thus eliminating the need for computers to a large extent.[38] Such mechanical and technological advancement would have not occurred if it was not through the enhancement of innovative ideas and revolutionary actions.

The second factor of individual achievements is competition. For individual action to fully reach its potential, it must be galvanized through competition. Only competition will make an individual do things that he would have never dared to do otherwise. When two parties compete for a reward, each party gives its maximum in order to win that reward. Although each party is vehemently

[36] Ibid.
[37] Ibid.
[38] Ibid.

stimulated to pursue its own self-interests, they each involuntarily produce great outcomes that benefit society as a whole because they produce greater output. As Adam Smith has expounded in *The Wealth of Nations* (1776), competition, which is encapsulated in the "invisible hand" of the free-market, makes individuals better off than worst off. Competition provides reassurance, builds loyalty, promotes improvement, and teaches new skills. The presence of competition means that consumers have the option to choose either your business or another business.[39] When there is competition, one knows that customers are using someone's business not because that person's business is the only one on the market, but because among the others out there, that person's business appealed to them the most.[40] Competition is important for someone's business

---

[39] McCormick, Kristen, "Why Is It Important for Companies To Have Competitors?" *Thrive Hive*, 2016, https://thrivehive.com/why-it-important-companies-have-competitors/. Article. Web.
[40] McCormick, Ibid.

because it provides reassurance that one is getting customers based of the quality of the products and services.[41] Competition does builds loyalty. Indeed, a customer is willing to remain loyal to a business insofar as the productivity of that business to which he is loyal to, continues to meet his needs. Furthermore, competition is utterly necessary because it incites improvement within the business. As a matter of fact, when the results of a business begin to shrink, it implies that the sales are not good, and the customers are therefore dissatisfied with the quality of service. So, the business owner is looking for solutions to improve the results otherwise the customers will buy the products of his competitor. Consequently, the business owner must change his strategy, and strengthen his human capital in order to deliver better outcomes. Competition prevents business owners to rest on their laurels and to keep working to improve their business strategies as

---

[41] McCormick, Ibid.

well as their resources. Lastly, competition promulgates the teachings and growth of new skills. Individual achievements in a free-market economy highly depend on the constant growth of skills. For the fact of the matter, it is important for an individual to continuously develop his skills because the market is based upon a spontaneous order whereby the course of events fluctuates from one momentum to another. It suggests that the actors who prompt the market must continuously update their skills in order to adapt to the realities of the market. That is why the teachings of new skills are an absolute necessity for a competitive market to follow its course.

The third factor that endows individual achievements is personal responsibility. Personal responsibility is a paramount component of individual achievements. Undoubtedly, personal responsibility matters in individual achievements because it is the element that accentuates on the value of human capital. The full embracement of personal responsibility is the main link that enables individuals to accumulate wealth. Moreover, I would say that personal responsibility is the psychological premise to end poverty. For example, an individual who wants to avoid poverty as he is growing up, must undertake the responsibility to have an education, to not have a child during his twenties if he is not married, or to be married before having a child, and must ensure to not have a criminal record. An individual who has at least a high school degree or a college degree, is eligible to be a competitive asset in the labor market. That same individual who does not have a child in his twenties, is enabled to become financially mature and responsible as he would be paying bills. Having a child after marriage strengthens the resources of the individual to earn a living. And having a criminal record eradicates all chances to obtain employment in the labor market. Only individual responsibility will determine the choices of an individual to either be economically emancipated or to remain in poverty. Only him has the power to make such decisions for himself. Furthermore, individual responsibility forces individuals to assume any risk in the pursuit of their endeavors. Decision is the precursor of human action, and results are only the consequences of that action. Incrementally, the personal responsibility of the individual is essential and necessary for the advancement of the free-market. When an individual embarks on entrepreneurship, he must first be aware of the risks he is taking. He must evaluate all the advantages and inconveniences of the project in which he wishes to undertake because a bad decision can lead to catastrophic financial outcomes. The degree of the results is based upon the extent of the decision. The larger the decision to undertake a humongous project is, the greater the risk of failure, and the pressure of responsibility accentuate upon the individual. Those who have revolutionized the world through their individual achievement such as Steve Jobs, Bill Gates, or Aliko Dangoté; ventured into enormous and costly projects in which the likelihood of failure was even greater. But the fact that they assumed the full responsibility for their actions ultimately delivered the results that they have seeded. The precept of personal responsibility generates leadership skills since leadership is about taking the risk to endeavor into something without necessarily knowing the ultimate outcome.

The fourth and last element that constitutes individual achievements in a free-market capitalistic system is family values. Karl Marx has always perceived marriage in a capitalist system as an extension of business. To an extent, he was not completely wrong because when two individuals got married, they merged their respective assets to expand their wealth. What could be more normal than that? Family values are important for personal achievements because when two married individuals increase the productivity of labor within the family, each of them maximizes his production so that the profit made remains in the family scope since the family is primarily a clan. In order to sustain and uphold the continuation of the accumulation of wealth within the family, parents educate their children on the principles and virtues of wealth and prepare them mentally to take upon the matter so that the creation of wealth continues to be stimulated within the familial scope. For example, the Kennedy Family is one of the wealthiest families in the United States because they amplified the wealth within the family scope. Joe Kennedy, Sr. was a wealthy man who married Rose Fitzgerald, the daughter of the Mayor of Boston, John Francis "Honey Fitz" Fitzgerald, who was one of the most prominent political figures in Massachusetts history and in the Irish community. The accumulation of wealth they both procreated was sustainable enough to feed at least two generations of Kennedy.

Chapter 3

PRIVATE OWNERSHIP vs. STATE OWNERSHIP

Let me commence this essay by asserting my vehement and unshakeable opposition to state ownership. State ownership ultimately leads to economic stagnation because individuals do not retain the means of production; and therefore, cannot innovate. It has been demonstrated throughout history that, when the state controls the means of production, it inevitably leads to economic stagnation then collapse. In socialist states like Cuba, Venezuela or the former Soviet Union; the government owns all means of production, which are managed by employees of the state.[42] These employees operate under party-appointed economic planners, who set output targets and prices and frequently interfered with the operations to satisfy personal or party desires.[43] And because communist and socialist economies are not efficient; and based on the fact that the State-party retains power, most economic resources are devoted to only strengthening the state's interests, which deprive consumers of food and other necessary products as well as of the freedom to purchase whatever they would like; causing intense competition for these limited and elemental necessities where many people had to wait in long lines for common consumer goods.[44] These factors enumerated are,

---

[42] *Economic System: Capitalism, Communism, and Socialism,* https://thismatter.com/economics/economic-systems.htm.
[43] Ibid.
[44] Ibid.

in fact, a reflection of a centrally-planned economy, also known as command economy.

On the philosophical aspect, state ownership is fundamentally wrong. It is even contrary to human nature and to the human condition. It is fundamentally contrary to human nature simply because human beings are intrinsically inclined to be individualistic. Men are driven by profit because profit is what determines the nature of self-preservation and self-ownership. It is subsequently conventional for a human being to retain the profit or the benefit of what he has produced. If an individual who has developed his skills for the sake of increasing the production of his labor in order to augment his wealth, why does the government or the state confiscate what has earned? It is unethical and morally wrong for the government to confiscate the rewards of someone's labor and to redistribute it to other individuals who did not put the work to earn their own assets. Common or communal property implies that personal efforts and individual fulfillment are worthless since the production of such efforts belong to an entity other than its author. A market economy in which the state exerts a substantial influence over the means of production, such as through the welfare state like in Continental Europe; the opportunities to expand the allocation of resources through the retention of private property are reduced. This reduction subsequently generates a scarcity in human capital, whereas it is human capital that develops the production of labor as well as the stimulation of wealth. Furthermore, compulsory redistribution of wealth is a sustainable method that empowers government to maintain control over the allocation of resources. When government raises income taxes, these compulsory taxes imposed on the wealthiest members of society and corporations, penalize the economy because it is the wealthiest members of society who hold the resources to incentive human capital. And state ownership forestalls such enhancement.

In the introduction, I vigorously defended capitalism by asseverating that it is a just and fair economic system whereby individuals are rewarded according to the value that they bring into the performance of their efforts. That is why the right to private property is the highest form of individual reward and the most fundamental right of the human condition. It is an absolute right because it is what man possesses in his own right and in absolute legality. Certainly, the right to private property is legitimate to the individual because it is the element that determines the value of man. To what extent is the individual willing to go in order to preserve his right to self-ownership? That simple question is the evidence which demonstrates the will power of man to go beyond the scope of his abilities to preserve that right. Capitalism is fair and moral because it recognizes the value of the individual. As a matter of fact, it is in a capitalistic free-market economy that men have the power and opportunity to fully demonstrate their full potential and abilities. Not in a centrally-planned economy where everything is centralized within the state, and opportunities are scarce.

According to libertarian thinker Robert Nozick, self-ownership is the right for an individual to have control over his person. The idea of self-ownership is attractive for many reasons.[45] People are recognized as self-owners when we recognize that there are things that may not be done to a person without their consent, which may be done without consent.[46] Thus, rape; for example; is wrong because it involves a body being used against the will of the person to whom it belongs, and not because there's something inherently wrong with the sexual intercourse.[47] Assault is also considered a wrongdoing for the

---

[45] "1. Self-Ownership", *Libertarianism,* (2002), substantive revision in 2018. Stanford Encyclopedia of Philosophy, https://plato.stanford.edu/entries/libertarianism/#SelOwn.
[46] Ibid.
[47] Ibid.

same reasons.[48] The principle of self-ownership is a strong endorsement of the moral importance and sovereignty of the individual, and it expresses the refusal to treat people as mere objects to be used or traded-off against each other. This same principal can be applied within the economic realm. State ownership is clearly a violation of private property because it violates the earnings of the individuals.

Private property and self-ownership are essential for the advancement of the human condition for three substantive reasons. In the book entitled *Elements of Moral Science*, Francis Wayland cogently identified the positive link between private property and human flourishing.[49] The first reason is based on the precept that private property allows the division of labor. The door to the division of labor is

---

[48] Ibid.

[49] Dr. Shawn Ritenour, "Three reasons Private Property Is Essential for Human Flourishing", *The Institute For Faith, Work & Economics*, (2014), https://tifwe.org/private-property-and-human-flourishing/. Article. Web.

opened by voluntary exchange because the possibility for exchange allows us to produce goods that are of service to others and not for merely for our own use.[50] And ownership is one of these institutions of the division of labor. People cannot exchange what they do not own.[51] In order to benefit from the economic development that flows from the division of labor, people must be secured in their property.[52] The second reason is premised on the principle of action that private property is necessary for capital formation. For people to have the incentive to accumulate capital, they must be secured in their property.[53] For example, the state enforces confiscatory taxation, and capital accumulation is hindered in two ways: (1) taxes increase the cost of production, reducing the net income from any business venture.[54] Additionally,

---

[50] Ritenour, Ibid.
[51] Ritenour, Ibid.
[52] Ritenour, Ibid.
[53] Ritenour, Ibid.
[54] Ritenour, Ibid.

people have less incentives to save and invest, because they are guaranteed a smaller return due to some of profit being away.[55] (2) Individuals are skeptical and discouraged from putting their savings at long-term risk if they are afraid that at any moment, it may be claimed by the government.[56] The social institution that makes saving and investment both possible and attractive is private property.[57] The third reason is grounded in the fact that private property is a necessary condition for wise entrepreneurship. In order to accumulate capital and other factors of production to be wisely stewarded and put toward their most valued uses, entrepreneurs use economic calculations based on money prices to determine profit or loss.[58] If entrepreneurs need money prices for economic calculation, it is obvious that society must have a monetary

---

[55] Ritenour, Ibid.
[56] Ritenour, Ibid.
[57] Ritenour, Ibid.
[58] Ritenour, Ibid.

economy rather than a fiscal one.[59] Furthermore, the money prices they use must be free market prices rather than government-mandated prices, because only prices are manifestations of the subjective values of the buyers and sellers in society.[60] A monetary economy facilitates the exchange and transfer of private property between individuals. The monetary economy is only adequate when it operates in a free-market economy. Private property incentives individuals to ameliorate the society they are living in.

---

[59] Ritenour, *Ibid.*
[60] Ritenour, *Ibid.*

Chapter 4

THE AUSTRIAN SCHOOL
vs.
THE CHICAGO SCHOOL

Among all the economic school of thoughts, the Austrian School of Economics and The Chicago School of Economics are the two main school of thoughts that advocate for a real laissez-faire capitalism and free-market economics. The main objectification of this essay is not to make a deliberate comparison of the two schools and declare which one is better than the other; but to simply offer the vision of two schools that have been promulgating and continue to do so, the greatest economic system that have enabled billions of individuals to be lifted out of poverty, to create wealth and to advance society as a whole. These two school of thoughts have continued to offer valuable theoretical inducements that contributed to the enhancement of modern economics. Both schools adamantly and uncompromisingly reject centrally-planned economy which promotes total government control of the means of production.

The principal difference between the two schools is in regard to the role of government in the economy. As a matter of fact, the Austrian School advocates for a total laissez-faire economy, which means a complete absence of government intervention in the economy, while the Chicago School preaches for a substantially limited government role in the economy. In other words, The Austrian School leans more towards anarcho-capitalism whereas the Chicago School does not entirely dismiss government intervention but believes that its role is and must be extremely minimal in the economy as well as social affairs.

The Austrian School argues that economic incentives in the free-market are driven by human action whilst the Chicago School maintains that the allocation of scarce resources determine economic incentives. Ludwig von Mises, one of the most prominent economists of the Austrian School, argued that the free-market operates best when it is driven by human action. He asserted that action is fundamental to what makes us human—that we are always in a state of "felt uneasiness," which we wish to remove through action.[61] Ludwig von Mises stressed that whatever actions we take and when we take them are determined by our own subjective judgments about the ends we wish to achieve and the best

---

[61] Horwitz, Steven, "On Human Action: We owe a debt to Ludwig von Mises", *Foundation for Economic Education*, (2012) https://fee.org/articles/on-human-action/. Article. Web.

means to achieve them.[62] According to Mises, the knowledge we have in our ideas is uniquely ours, and it informs how we value ends and means.[63] Since human action is the primary denominator of economic incentives, it suggests that it is human action that determines monetary value and the price of production.[64] There is nothing mechanical or automatic about this process; rather it requires conscious action. This subjective process from knowledge to valuation to choice-in-action is the starting point of all economic analysis for the Austrian School.[65] What markets make possible is nothing less than social cooperation—for Mises, the division of labor and the specialization process is not only the source of economic growth and the improvement of billions of human lives, it is also the source of deeper human bonds. Markets induce individuals to cooperate rather than plunder, and in so doing,

---

[62] Horwitz, Ibid.
[63] Horwitz, Ibid.
[64] Horwitz, Ibid.
[65] Horwitz, Ibid.

help to create peaceful civilizations.[66] It is important to remember that the will precedes the action. That being said, the Austrian School argues that the will is the harbinger of definite human action. The will enables individuals to voluntarily associate themselves to one another in order to effectuate trades freely. Free economic association and fully guaranteed policy even to design our own governments and economics since they are not the aggressors of the peaceful coexistence of rights of other persons and societies of peace.[67]

The Chicago School of Economics stipulates that the free-market works best when the resources are allocated and when there is a minimal or even no government intervention. The Chicago School includes monetarist beliefs about

---

[66] Horwitz, Ibid.
[67]Brancaglione, Marcus, "Free Market, Free Will, Self-Regulation", *Medium Co*, (2015), https://medium.com/@mbrancaglione/free-market-free-will-self-regulation-c6a1396bb534. Article. Web.

the economy, contending that the money supply should be kept in equilibrium with the demand for money.[68] Milton Friedman, the most famous economist in American history, and legendary pioneer of the University of Chicago School of Economics; argued that economic freedom was a necessary condition for political freedom. To Friedman and the Chicago School, the individual is the best judge of his own interests and maintained that government had to do something about third-party effects of individual actions, but if it went beyond that, government was doing more harm than good.[69] Unlike the Austrian School which advocates for a complete absence of the state in the economy, economists of the Chicago School articulate that we do still need government to protect our property rights, to enforce contract, local safety, and the national defense. The Chicago School has always relied on

---

[68] Kenton, Will, "Chicago School" *Investopedia*, (2018), https://www.investopedia.com/terms/c/chicago_school.asp

[69] Kenton, Ibid.

mathematical symbols and operations to determine the promulgation of the free-market. Friedman's quantity theory of money holds that general price levels in the economy are determined by the amount of money in circulation.[70] By managing general price levels, economic growth can be better controlled in a world where individuals and groups make economic allocations decisions in a rational way.[71]

Although both schools advocate for free-market economics, the most important difference between the two are their completely differing theories on how to draw conclusions in economics. The Chicago School which sits squarely in the mainstream culture, advocates

---

[70] McCurray, John, "Economist Milton Friedman Championed Free Markets and Individualism", *Investor's Business Daily*, (2016), https://www.investors.com/news/management/leaders-and-success/economist-milton-friedman-championed-free-markets-and-individualism/. Article. Web.

[71] McCurray, Ibid.

empiricism as it applies to economics, acknowledging the merits of positivism and mathematical reasoning.[72] Thus, members of the Chicago School utilize models in order to draw conclusions, much like other mainstream economists.[73] The Austrian School is considered heterodox due to its methodology.[74] Austrian economists, following the teachings of Ludwig von Mises, believe that empirical reasoning cannot be used to analyze the largely unpredictable course of human action.[75] Rather, they argue that pure logic is the only tool by which the science of economics can advance, for

---

[72] Kenton, Will, "Chicago School" *Investopedia*, (2018), https://www.investopedia.com/terms/c/chicago_school.asp .

[73] Kenton, Ibid.

[74] "Chicago School vs. Austrian School: Battle of the Free-marketeers", *The Economic Review*, September 24, 2011, https://theeconomicreview.wordpress.com/2011/09/24/chicago-school-vs-austrian-school-battle-of-the-free-marketeers/. Article. Web.

[75] Ibid.

it is the only way to deduce the ways in which humans will act.[76] Moreover, the Austrian economists reject positivism and the idea that economics is largely a mathematical science, and most of their arguments are verbal.[77] Chicago School economists agree with Austrians on microeconomics issues simply because their mathematical models confirm the validity of the free-market on the premise of supply and demand.[78] On the other hand, Chicago School economists support government action on a macroeconomic scale for the same reason, a perceived empirical validity.[79]

---

[76] Ibid.
[77] Ibid.
[78] Ibid.
[79] Ibid.

Chapter 5

MONETARY POLICY AND INFLATION

Every economic system has a monetary policy, a fiscal policy, and a system of inflation. The free-market does not escape this rule. It is actually a necessary condition for economic freedom to fully thrive. In the free-market system, the fundamental issue in banking and monetary policy is whether government can improve monetary institutions of the unhampered market.[80] All government intervention in this field boils down to schemes that increase the quantity of money beyond what it otherwise would be.[81] The libertarian case for the abolishment of government intervention in money and banking rests on the insight that the latter serves only redistributive purposes.[82] Monetary policy is concerned with modifications of the quantity of money.[83] For example, to reduce short-term interest rates, policymakers must be in a position to produce additional quantities of money and offer them on the so-called money market, lest they cannot exercise any downward pressure on rates at all.[84]

In the free-market, every individual would have the right to invest his labor and his property

[80] Hülsmann, Jörg Guido, "Monetary Policy and the Free Market", *Mises Daily Articles,* The Mises Institute, (2003), https://mises.org/library/monetary-policy-and-free-market. Article. Web.
[81] Hülsmann, *Ibid.*
[82] Hülsmann, *Ibid.*
[83] Hülsmann, *Ibid.*
[84] Hülsmann, *Ibid.*

in the production of money and to sell or give away his product as himself seems fit.[85] Every money producer would, in this sense, pursue his own monetary policy, just as each shoe manufacturer in selling his product pursues his own "foot fashion policy."[86] Free-market economists are in favor of monetary policy over fiscal policy because monetary policy enables the expansion of money quantity. Those who oppose such changes depend on whether the problems associated with moving to a lower price level are worse than the problems created by monetary institutions that generate an increase in the nominal quantity of money supply.[87] The main feature of monetary policy in a free-market economy is rooted in the fact that money prices, which include the prices of resources, such as the

---

[85] Hülsmann, *Ibid.*

[86] Hülsmann, *Ibid.*

[87] Woolsey, Bill, "Free Market Economists and Monetary Policy", *Monetary Freedom,* (2010). http://monetaryfreedom-billwoolsey.blogspot.com/2010/11/bryan-caplan-asks-why-free-market.html. Article. Web.

wages paid to labor, must decrease enough to raise the real quantity of money to match the demand to hold the money.[88] The reduction in the price level will raise real expenditures on goods and services enough to match the productive capacity of the economy.[89] As monetary policy is substantively and fundamentally different from fiscal policy, it impacts the important facets of the economy, which include attempts to achieve the stability of the Gross Domestic Product (GDP) growth, maintain low rates of unemployment, support overall economic or sector specific growth, and maintain foreign exchange rates in a predictable range.[90] For example, if a country is facing a high unemployment rate during a slowdown or a recession, the monetary authority can opt for expansionary policy which is aimed at

---

[88] Woolsey, *Ibid.*
[89] Woolsey, *Ibid.*
[90] Chen, James, "Monetary Policy, *Investopedia,* (2018). https://www.investopedia.com/terms/m/monetarypolicy.asp.

bumping up the economic growth and expanding the overall economic activity in the region.[91]

In a free-market economy, what truly matters for economic stimulation, is the availability of capital. As capital is available at lower rates and on short-term basis, both businesses and individuals can take loans on convenient terms.[92] This aspect reflects the voluntary exchange occurring between two entities—whether it is an exchange between two individuals, two businesses, or an exchange between an individual and a business entity. Furthermore, monetary policy favors investment through individual action rather than government spending through tax cuts. The contractionary monetary policy can slow the economic growth and increase unemployment but is often required to tame inflation.[93]

---

[91] Chen, *Ibid.*
[92] Chen, *Ibid.*
[93] Chen, *Ibid.*

What is inflation? Inflation is when the prices of goods and services increase.[94] There are four main types of inflation, as they are categorized by their speed.[95] These types are Creeping Inflation, Walking Inflation, Galloping Inflation and Hyperinflation.[96] The first, which is the *Creeping Inflation*, is when prices rise by 2 percent a year or less.[97] According to the Federal Reserve, when prices increase by 2 percent, or less, it benefits economic growth—it makes consumers expect that prices will keep going up, which boost demand.[98] The second, which is the *Walking Inflation*, is the most pernicious within the free-market. Prices increase between 3 and 10 percent a year.[99] It is harmful to the economy

---

[94] Amadeo, Kimberly, "Types of Inflation: The Four Most Critical Plus Nine More: Including Asset, Wage, and Core Inflation", *The Balance,* December 22, 2018, https://www.thebalance.com/types-of-inflation-4-different-types-plus-more-3306109. Article. Web.

[95] Amadeo, *Ibid.*

[96] Amadeo, *Ibid.*

[97] Amadeo, *Ibid.*

[98] Amadeo, *Ibid.*

[99] Amadeo, *Ibid.*

because it heats up economic growth too fast.[100] Walking Inflation intensifies demands because consumers purchase more than they need. The third kind of inflation, which is the *Galloping Inflation* occurs when prices of goods and services rise to over 10 percent. When it reaches this point, money commences to lose value so fast that businesses and employee income cannot keep up with costs and prices.[101] Under a Galloping Inflation, the economy becomes unstable, and government leaders lose credibility.[102] The fourth and last type of inflation is *Hyperinflation*. Hyperinflation is the worst kind of inflation—it implies that prices skyrocket at more than 50 percent a month.[103] In fact, most examples of hyperinflation have occurred only when governments printed money to pay for wars— Zimbabwe and Venezuela are two examples of

---

[100] Amadeo, *Ibid.*
[101] Amadeo, *Ibid.*
[102] Amadeo, *Ibid.*
[103] Amadeo, *Ibid.*

hyperinflation and economic collapse.[104] In a free-market system, Creeping Inflation is the best kind of inflation because the rise of prices and goods and services is a healthy cycle. Prices need to rise once in a while in order to stimulate demand. Inflation is not a predicament unless it rises above 3 percent of prices' increase.

The Great Depression empowered the theories of British economist John Maynard Keynes to take place, which epitomized more government intervention and regulations of business cycles. Capitalism is a complete and natural economic system which regulates itself because prices adjust themselves based on demand. When government intervenes to regulate the economy through fiscal policy and taxation, it intrinsically reduces economic opportunities, destabilizes the price system, and imposes conformity. By conformity, I mean that businesses are not unconditionally free to conduct

---

[104] Amadeo, *Ibid.*

their business as they wish or see fit. They are compelled to follow a set of rules laws imposed by the state. Government intervention subverts voluntary association and free will because individuals are coerced to pay an amount of taxation that does not necessarily equate the outcome of the production of their labor. As they are compelled to tax's subjection, their contingency to control prices and demand is also reduced.

As fiscal policy is the use of government spending and taxation to influence the economy, when the government takes control of the goods and services it purchases, the transfer payments it distributes or the taxes it collects; it affects the aggregate level of output by changing the incentives that firms (businesses) or individuals face.[105] Fiscal policy changes the composition of

---

[105] Weil, David, "Fiscal Policy", *The Library of Economics and Liberty,* 2018, https://www.econlib.org/library/Enc/FiscalPolicy.html. Article.

aggregate demand.[106] When government runs a deficit, it meets some of its expenses by issuing bonds. In doing so, it competes with private borrowers for money loaned by savers.[107] Since fiscal policy concentrates on taxation, its expansion inevitably raises interest rates, which subsequently reduces private investment. In a free-market economy, fiscal policy also affects the exchange rate and the trade balance.[108] In the case of fiscal expansion, the rise in interest rates due to government borrowing attracts foreign capital,[109] but has an impact on local private investors. In their attempt to get more dollars to invest, foreigners bid up the price of the dollar, causing exchange-rate appreciation in the short-run.[110] This appreciation makes imported goods

---

[106] Weil, *Ibid.*
[107] Weil, *Ibid.*
[108] Weil, *Ibid.*
[109] Weil, *Ibid.*
[110] Weil, *Ibid.*

cheaper in the United States and exports more expensive abroad.[111]

Overall, fiscal policy, which is an element of the entire Keynesian economics' package, is part of the short-term outcome of government intervention. For a free-market capitalist society to run efficiently and on long-term basis, it must rely on monetary authority over fiscal policy. The reason for that statement is simply that since the free-market is a spontaneous order embodied by human action, it fixes itself during times of economic recession through the continuation of human action. The problem with government intervention in the free-market is that once government is involved, it does not withdraw after it has fulfilled its task. It becomes a permanent regulator of the economy and continues to grow its authority over decision-making.

---

[111] Weil, *Ibid.*

If an economy is controlled by government regulation and that economy falls into a recession, government will expand the problem instead of abrogating it. It will require an excessive rise of income taxation in order to create a new government agency that will attempt to solve the problem. More licenses, tariffs, and regulations will be invigorated by the government, which legitimately reduce economic incentives and the creation of wealth.

PART II

THE POLITICAL
PHILOSOPHY
OF
THE FREE-MARKET

Chapter 6

FREEDOM OF THOUGHT AND FREEDOM OF ACTION

"To achieve, you need thought. You have to know what you are doing and that's the real power"[112]

Ayn Rand

Among all the living beings that populate and constitute our planet, the individual is the highest being among all. What differentiates the individual from animals, insects, and plants; is

---

[112] Quote By Ayn Rand

the fact that the individual has the ability to think. The ability to think implies that a living being has the power to formulate, process, and execute a course of action through a rational psychological perception. Some animals, such as felines, hyenas, reptiles (crocodiles and snakes) or sharks are predators; not because they developed the ability to become predators but because these animals were procreated that way; based upon a biological mechanism which determined the natural component that enables them to exercise their predatory behavior when they chase their prey. The way in which predatory animals pursue their prey is not grounded on a thoughtful and formulated mechanism in which the chase takes place. It is merely based on instinct; a strong innate sense that reason is unable to control, and instinct is not a feature of rationality. So, predatory animals do not voluntarily, and through a rational psychological process; chase their prey. They chase their prey out of survival instinct because they need to feed themselves in order to survive, otherwise they will die if they do not. Such mechanism is based upon the natural law by which predatory animals instinctively abide by. This is why animals do live in the state of nature; a state in which rules, regulations, and customs are quintessentially absent because reason does not exist in such world. The individual, however, is the only living being on planet Earth, since its creation, who has the ability to think. Man has the power to formulate, to process, and to execute the course of action through a rational psychological perception. As man has the capacity to distinguish between right and wrong; and good and evil; he is, then, a moral agent of his own will. We shall remember that animals do not kill out of cruelty while men do choose to do evil if they want to since they have that capacity and ability to do so whether is psychological or physical.

The primary, the foremost and elemental freedom of the individual, is his liberty to think because he has the innate ability to do so. Thought is precisely the very first wealth of man because it is from the capacity to think that individuals have the ability to create, to transform and to even destroy. Thought is the main factor that determines the creation of a man-made entity. No one, no being or entity can circumvent an individual to think because thought is ingrained in the brain of every human being. The power to think gives man the power to convert the abstract into the real; to materialize perception and cognition into a finished product. The power of thinking legitimizes the will of human action because human action is preceded by thought whether it is premeditated or involuntary. The freedom to think is indeed the real factor that enables the improvement and progress of the human condition through the evolution of time. The transition from an archaic, rudimentary and agricultural world into a modern, industrialized, and technological world; took place principally during the Industrial Revolution where individuals who used, then, rudimentary tools, began to utilize mechanical tools to increase the production of labor powers. The transition of such system was first operated by the freedom of thought before being physically effectuated. If the individual were deprived of his liberty to think, the world in which we live today would have been a rudimentary, archaic, and outmoded world; without laws and social values, a world wherein the rule of the stronger would have prevailed over the consent of the governed, of the individual, the free will of the individual, voluntary association, and civility. The freedom to think stimulates the perpetual improvement of the human condition.

In a capitalistic system where the means of production are held by private actors of the economy, freedom of thought is the foremost; the principal axis of economic stimulation and the creation of capital as well as wealth. Freedom of thought is essential in a free-market economy because innovation, psychological development and the maximization of skills; originated from the formulation of ideas that individuals apply to real factual situations once these ideas have been formulated and diligently processed. That is why entrepreneurs, although they are considered pragmatists because of their efficacy; are primarily thinkers. The great events that have shaped the world, have all sprouted from thought. For example, Steve Jobs is considered one of the greatest entrepreneurs of all times for computerizing cell phones. The creation of the iPhone has revolutionized the modern world forever because Steve Jobs has expanded the functionalities of the cell phone beyond its primary role, which were simply to make phone calls, send and receive text messages. People can now use the iPhone as a Global Positioning System (GPS) to locate themselves within an unknown geographical area; to save their files and documents; or to check their health condition even before booking an appointment to the doctor. Such innovation has simplified and facilitated human effort. If Steve Jobs was able to influence the world by the creation of the iPhone and all other technological devices through Apple Incorporation, which have improved the human condition as well as they have created more employment opportunities in the labor market; it is thanks to his ability to think in a laissez-faire capitalist system. His [Steve Jobs] freedom of thought enabled him to promulgate his innovative ideas into his individual action which benefited society as whole. Jobs would have been unable to effectuate his ideas if the United States was a socialist country because the central planners would have owned the production of his works. Steve Jobs is not the only entrepreneur who has revolutionized the world. Henry Ford, the Wright Brothers, Albert Einstein, Bill Gates, Louis Pasteur, John D. Rockefeller and many other prominent entrepreneurs, have stimulated, changed, and shaped the world for the better through their ideas and actions.

Socialism is the greatest enemy of liberty. As socialism is an economic and political system in which the government controls the means of production as well as the lives of the citizens, it disenfranchises the individual from all forms of liberty including the freedom to think. That is why any country that has tried socialism, has miserably failed economically and has become politically a tyranny where government control was absolute and omnipotent. Socialism is an open prison in which the individual is arbitrarily and perpetually condemned to be a slave of government's authority. Socialism as a doctrine is much deeper than the mere control of the means of production by the government. Socialism aims at eradicating the essence of the individual which is his freedom of thought; his ability to think by himself and for himself. The two ways whereby socialism aims at suppressing individual thinking are by the regulation of morality, and by compulsory collectivism. Both elements go together. The regulation of morality is a way for the government to control the behavior of the individual. By imposing a certain policy based on moral premises as law, government becomes the arbitrator which determines what is right from what is wrong, what is good from what is bad; whereas only the individual is the master of his own will as well as of his actions, and the only judge of his conscience. Regulating morality is based upon altruism. Every means of implementing government control commands individuals to be altruistic, selfless, and to become their brother's keeper. The act of caring for the well-being of someone else should be voluntary rather than compulsory. When individuals are motivated by altruism, their ability to think coherently, innovatively, and competitively; reduces the incentives for personal emancipation. Adherence to altruism unavoidably generates individual guilt. For example, an individual feels guilty for not having satisfied the needs of the other person and he tells himself that he is a terrible person for not helping the other. Such sentiment hampers the liberty to think because the individual no longer thinks about his own well-being but is rather concerned about the fear of being judged by others. And such sentiment is reciprocal among people at creating a common way of thinking instead of having human beings thinking independently. Socialism utilizes morality to control individual thinking and transcends such utility into groupthink and collectivism. Tyranny arises when groupthink prevails over individual thinking because demagogues can easily use and do utilize collective judgment to rise to power and suppress individual liberties. For example, Soviet Russia was founded on altruism. Lenin, who was its leader from 1917 to 1924; concentrated and consolidated power by regulating morality. The kind of morality Lenin administered on Soviet Russians was not the establishment of a national religion, but a compulsory perception of obedience to the Soviet state. It entails that any individual who lived in Soviet Russia at that time was compelled to prioritize the interests of the state before his own self-interests. And if an individual did not exercise altruism towards the collective interests of Soviet Russia, he was classified as a traitor and as a counter-revolutionary to the state and therefore ought to be punished by state power; whether this individual was murdered by the political police or enslaved in the Gulag during the reign of Stalin. The regulation of morality is a political technique that allows to maintain the subjugation of the individual to the authority of the state because if an individual is free to think for himself, then he becomes a danger to the collective interest.

Compulsory collectivism, on the other hand, is when a government controls the means of production and imposes social policies on individuals to force them to assemble their individual productions of labor to the benefit of the state. In a socialistic society, the state controls the means of production. It signifies that the state is the earner of the production of labor that has been effectuated by the effort and achievement of the individual. In a socialist state, the individual is not rewarded at his just value for his contributive effort to the productivity of the economy since his essence is insignificant compared to that of the state. It implies that the individual is a mere tool, who is occupying an auxiliary and subordinating role to the economic growth. Furthermore, the regulation of morality enhances compulsory collectivism because it leads to the abandonment or the confiscation of private property and self-ownership. If the individual is deprived of his property, and his liberty, then what remains of him? If the individual has no longer the right to think for himself, then what value does he bring to the community? To dispossess him of his liberty of thought is to deprive him of his essence as a human being and as an individual. To deprive an individual of his liberty of thought, is to reduce him to the animal stage where only savagery, barbarism and the survival instinct prevail.

If capitalism is an economic system which has been proven to be effective and beneficial to society as a whole, it is because individuals living under a capitalist system are free to think and thus free to convert their ideas into action; free to materialize the conceptualization of their ideas into finished products. Individual achievement can only occur when individuals are free to cooperate voluntarily; free from state intervention and coercion. When individuals pursue their economic self-interests by voluntarily cooperating with one another, they unintentionally contribute to economic growth as well as to the improvement of the human condition as a whole.

Chapter 7

INDIVIDUAL RIGHTS

Individual rights, according to the *Business Dictionary*, is the freedom to act, work, think and behave without retribution bestowed upon members of an organization through legal, regulatory and societal standards.[113] I can also define it as a set of rights attributed to an individual who is a member of a civil society. Most liberal democracies such as those of the United States, the United Kingdom, Canada, Australia, France or Germany; are political

---

[113] "Individual Rights", *Business Dictionary*. http://www.businessdictionary.com/definition/individual-rights.html.

regimes based on the laws and the respect place upon the freedom of the individual. By the "freedom of the individual," I do not mean that the individual can do whatever he wants, whenever it pleases him, in a reckless manner— because such behavior will automatically and inevitably encroach the freedom of others and will certainly endanger their well-being. By the "freedom of the individual" I mean that an individual within a civil society, is free to choose and pursue his own values and interests as he sees fit, so long as he does not infringe the rights and liberty of others.

Aristotle is considered to be the founder of the philosophy of individualism and John Locke is considered to be the father of liberal democracy; and the two are fundamentally philosophically related. Liberal democracies are systems of government that prioritize individual rights and personal responsibility as the main factors of political, economic and social liberalism. Individualism and liberal democracy are linked to one another because one reflects the means and the other reflects the end. The fundamental virtue of individualism is the pursuit of happiness, which means the fulfillment of the individual. This concept advocated by Aristotle in *Nicomachean Ethics* (1791) enshrines happiness as the central purpose of human life and a goal in itself.[114] So, happiness is the end, the finality, the destination wherein the individual is heading toward. The rights of the individual are the means by which the individual is legitimately entitled to fulfill that happiness; and this concept is championed by John Locke in his book *Second Treatise of Government* (1689). Locke argued that such rights cannot be violated by any external entity because they are inalienable. By inalienable, Locke implied that these rights are solely unique to the individual because it is the individual who consents and who delegates his

---

[114] "Introduction: Aristotle's Definition of Happiness", *Aristotle,* The pursuit of Happiness-Bringing the Science of Happiness To Life, https://www.pursuit-of-happiness.org/history-of-happiness/aristotle/.

rights to government. Government is only the agent that protects the inalienable rights of the individual within his pursuit of happiness. As individual fulfillment is the end and individual rights are the means to reach this end; it is fair then to asseverate that individualism and liberal democracy are intimately linked since a liberal democracy is indeed a free and civil society, and a free society is founded on the fulfillment of the individual. To have the right to do something means to have the freedom to do that thing. According to John Locke, the individual is entitled to three fundamental inalienable rights which are the right to life, which means that the individual is the sole master and decider of his own life; the right to liberty, which means that the individual is free to live his life as he sees fit so long as he does not encroach the rights of others; and the right to property, which means that the individual is entitled to secure his own person and property and whatever goods he has acquired. These three fundamental rights constitute the groundwork of individual liberties; and are also the basis of the functioning of a so-called "free society."

Individual rights are an essential element and a necessary condition for the functioning of capitalism and a free-market economy. In order for individuals to freely contribute to economic growth, they must be protected by their rights. Without individual rights; human capital, voluntary trades, economic incentives, the increase of the production of labor, individual achievements and the creation of wealth; cannot take place in a capitalist society and it can never take place in a centralized economy. Capitalism, as Ayn Rand properly defined it in her book *Capitalism: The Unknown Ideal*, (1966), is "a social system based on the recognition of individual rights, including property rights, in which all property is privately owned."[115]

---

[115] Salsman, Richard M. "Individual Rights and The Essential Nature of Capitalism", *Capitalism Magazine*, (1999)https://www.capitalismmagazine.com/1999/12/individual-rights-and-the-essential-nature-of-capitalism/. Article. Web.

Capitalism is not a system that permits the violation of individual rights.[116] It is a system of objective laws, laws that are just, clearly defined and known in advance, laws that protect individual rights—the only kind of rights that exist—including rights to private property.[117] That means the right to one's property, to the property he has earned—is not some alleged "right" to the property of others, involuntarily surrendered.[118] Objective laws are just laws, laws that punish evil and protect the good,[119] laws that are based upon the reward of just value or pure worthiness. According to Ayn Rand, capitalism is not today's system, with a mixture of freedom and government control, but a social system, in which the government is exclusively devoted to the protection of individual rights—one in which there is absolutely no government intervention in

---

[116] Salsman, Ibid.
[117] Salsman, Ibid.
[118] Salsman, Ibid.
[119] Salsman, Ibid.

the economy.[120] The principal moral ethical code of capitalism is individual rights. As rights are a moral concept—the concept that provides a logical transition from the principles guiding an individual's action to the principles guiding his relationship with others—the concept that preserves and protects individual morality in a social context—the link between the moral code of a man and the legal code of society, between ethics and politics.[121] As every political system is grounded to an extent on a code of ethics, these codes of ethics shall, in fact, strengthen the rights of the individual for the latter to achieve happiness; and individual fulfillment. The principle of man's individual rights represented the extension of morality into the social system— as a limitation on the power of the state, as man's

---

[120] Rand, Ayn, *Capitalism: The Unknown Ideal,* 1966, Ayn Rand Institute, https://www.aynrand.org/novels/capitalism-the-unknown-ideal.
[121] Rand, Ayn, "Man's Rights", *The Virtue of Selfishness,* (1963), https://ari.aynrand.org/issues/government-and-business/individual-rights. Essay.

protection against the brute force of the collective, as the subordination of might to right.[122]

The United States regarded man as an end in himself, and society as a means to the peaceful, orderly, voluntary coexistence of individuals.[123] The American political culture held that man's life is his by right, that a right is the property of an individual, that society as such has no rights, and that the only moral purpose of a government is the protection of individual rights.[124] Libertarians elevate personal freedom to the highest good—as an end to be achieved.[125] Freedom is viewed as a prerequisite to the achievement of any of man's goals.[126] The self-ownership principle creates a zone of privacy and freedom of action for each

---

[122] Rand, Ibid.
[123] Rand, Ibid.
[124] Rand, Ibid.
[125] Younkins, Edward, "Perspective on Capitalism and Freedom: The Proper Role of The State is Limited", *Foundation For Ecoomic Education*, 1996, https://fee.org/articles/perspectives-on-capitalism-and-freedom/.
[126] Younkins, Ibid.

individual.[127] It suggests that when dealing with others each persons should respect them as equals in moral status and human dignity who have the right and responsibility to make their own decision regarding their own life, property, body, energies and speech.[128] Capitalism enables individuals to live their lives as they see fit and to have their rights protected. Additionally, since the individual's happiness is the standard value of man's worth, the best way for man to preserve that value is if state's intervention is excessively minimal to quasi non-existent. Because force is the means by which one's rights are violated, it follows that freedom is a fundamental social good.[129] The role of government is to protect man's natural rights, through the use of force but only in retaliation and only against those who initiate its use.[130] Nowadays, in the current liberal democracies we have, individual rights are not as

---

[127] Younkins, Ibid.
[128] Younkins, Ibid.
[129] Younkins, Ibid.
[130] Younkins, Ibid.

prominent anymore because of a substantial government's encroachment in the economy. The mixed economies, which reflect capitalism on the one hand, and government intervention on the other hand; that are currently ruling the western hemisphere; are favoring more government intervention than the preservation of individual rights. And such political magnitude places the individual in an uncomfortable situation where the protection of his rights is becoming exponentially fragile as they are exposed to a greater threat of government infringement upon his liberty. Most European nations are especially social democracies because their mixed economies give more power to their government to regulate economic activities over letting individuals pursuing their own self-interests. It is significantly urgent for liberal democracies to readopt and reaffirm the principles of laissez-faire economics, where the free-market reigns as the absolute and indispensable economic system which thoroughly secures the rights of the individual. It is within a laissez-faire economy that the individual is free to the fullest.

Chapter 8

LIMITED GOVERNMENT

Capitalism cannot adequately germinate if government is not substantially limited. It indicates that a limited government is a necessary condition for free-market capitalism to properly function. Individual achievement cannot occur if the state is substantively involved in the citizen's life. The very purpose of laissez-faire economics is to leave the individual alone; free from any form of coercion, to let him pursue what stimulates him, drives him, and makes him valuable. When the authority of government is not restricted, it incentivizes a great danger upon the liberty of the individual. As a matter of fact, government intervention is detrimental for laissez-faire economics because it limits the human potential to create capital, opportunity, and wealth. And the individual is the driving factor that enhances these elements within a laissez-faire economy. It is for these specific reasons that individual liberty is characteristically and unconditionally imperative in order to promote and further the advancement of society and the betterment of the human condition. The more government intervenes in the economy, the more economic opportunities are reduced, and the more individual liberties are violated.

It is interesting to witness to what extent liberal democracies, which are initially and properly speaking free-market economies; have drastically adopted a more interventionist, a more invasive, a more intrusive, and a more

"Keynesian" approach to the economy. The problem of mixed economies is based upon the fact that the balance between the role of government in the economy and that of private actors is not exacted. There is no precise middle ground between the two because one weights more power than the other. Government exercises a substantial influence and authority over the means of production. It subsidizes some businesses whether it is partially or entirely. Yet it does not entail that our liberal democracies have necessarily become socialist regimes, but it substantiated that the government; from having a temporary role in the economy, which is generally due to economic recessions; has transitioned into a permanent role in the economy. The main threat about permanent government intervention is that it will inevitably lead to total government control. Scandinavia, for instance, which is composed of its countries which are Denmark, Norway, Sweden, Finland, and Iceland; has adopted a social democracy, a kind of mixed economy in which government retains a considerable portion of ownership and the means of production. So far, the concept of a mixed economy in Scandinavia has been overall felicitous although it has already proven its limits. Social industries such as education, health, and infrastructures are supplied by government action rather than by private actors. The question remains whether the so-called "success" of this economic method will remain indefinite. One of the reasons why social democracy operates well enough in Scandinavia; is because its population is undersized. For example, as of January 2019, Denmark has a population of 5, 756, 387 inhabitants;[131] Norway has a population of 5,378,469 inhabitants;[132] Sweden has a population of 10,019,907

---

[131] "Denmark Population" http://www.worldometers.info/world-population/denmark-population/

[132] "Norway Population" http://www.worldometers.info/world-population/norway-population/

inhabitants;[133] Finland has a population of 5,552,494 inhabitants;[134] and Iceland has a population of 339, 251 inhabitants.[135] Indeed, each of these countries has a relatively small population compared to that of the United States or the United Kingdom; or even France. Since Scandinavian nations have comparatively undersized population, it is easier for their governments to supply goods and services to their inhabitants. The small population in Scandinavian nations enables their governments to have an easier control of the means of production and to retain ownership than in its western counterparts.

Among all liberal democracies, the United States is the country where laissez-faire

---

[133] "Sweden Population" http://www.worldometers.info/world-population/sweden-population/

[134] "Finland Population" http://www.worldometers.info/world-population/finland-population/

[135] "Iceland Population" http://www.worldometers.info/world-population/iceland-population/

economics is the most in danger. The adherents and defenders of the principles of the theory of Keynesian economics; advocated for a government which is more interventionist than it has already been. It is a premonitory danger for individual liberties in the United States because the American constitution was notably based upon the concept of liberty. A concept wherein the value of the individual prevails and of which the essence of the individual is sovereign. In order to preserve this sovereignty of the individual, the Founding Fathers have established in the Constitution; the Bill of Rights; a set of rights that protects the physical, economic, political, and social integrity of the individual against the coercive power of the central government. Besides the protection of individual rights, the Bill of Rights has played two fundamental roles within its aim to preserve the sovereignty of the individual. First, it clearly defined the constitutional scope upon which the federal government was legitimized to exercise its authority; and second, it has established the capitalistic nature of American culture in its perception of the human condition. Nearly two centuries before Ludwig von Mises and Friedrich August von Hayek popularized the principles of Austrian economic theory, James Madison was espousing the same view, call it the Virginia economic theory.[136] As stated very plainly in the Declaration of Independence, "Government are instituted among Men, deriving their just powers from the consent of the governed."[137] This brief explication of the rights of Americans restrains legitimate government with two very powerful fetters: the ends of government which must be to secure our natural rights; and the means it uses to achieve that end, which must be consented to by the people.[138] As James Madison understood,

---

[136] Wolverton, Joe, "James Madison and Limited Government", *New American-That Freedom Shall Not Perish,*(2010), https://www.thenewamerican.com/culture/history/item/4781-james-madison-and-limited-government. Article. Web.

[137] Wolverton, *Ibid.*

[138] Wolverton, *Ibid.*

government exists simply to secure the rights which nature and nature's God had endowed the individual.[139] The wide plain of human existence was to be unhemmed by fences of government intervention.[140]

Furthermore, James Madison attached the constitutional scope of government to the principles of "enumerated powers." The basic definition of enumerated powers is that the best limitation on power is to not give it in the first place.[141] According to Madison, government powers were legitimate if they had been granted to the government by the people and written specifically in the document through which the governed gave life to the government and the Constitution.[142] The fact of having a government significantly limited suggests that the individual has more liberty to live his life as he sees fit. The Bill of Rights has largely contributed to define the

---

[139] Wolverton, *Ibid.*
[140] Wolverton, *Ibid.*
[141] Wolverton, *Ibid.*
[142] Wolverton, *Ibid.*

original capitalistic mindset of the American people at the dawn of the republic. The Founders' approach to economics, when it is discussed by public figures and intellectuals, has been criticized.[143] One reason many on the Left reject the Founders' economic theory is that they think it encourages selfishness and leads to an unjust distribution of wealth.[144] Private ownership is one of the fundamental elements of the Bill of Rights that developed the capitalistic nature of the American people. Government must define who owns what, allow property to be used as each owner deems best, encourage widespread ownership among citizens, and protect property against infringements by others, including unjust infringement by government itself.[145] Using

---

[143] West, Thomas, "The Economic Principles of America's Founders: Property Rights, Free Markets, and Sound Money", *The Heritage Foundation,* (2010), https://www.heritage.org/political-process/report/the-economic-principles-americas-founders-property-rights-free-markets-and. Article. Web.
[144] West, *Ibid.*
[145] West, *Ibid.*

government coercion to redistribute property certainly violates the natural right to possess property.[146] Unless the possessors voluntarily choose to spread their wealth around, those who are starving will have no way of getting what they need except by theft or violence.[147] The emphasis on property rights settled the path to a free-market. With some exceptions, everyone must be free to sell anything to anyone at any time or place at any mutually agreeable price.[148] Government must define and enforce contracts.[149] To facilitate market transactions, there must be a medium of exchange whose value is reasonably constant and certain.[150] Government officials can deprive someone of property just as effectively as fellow citizens or foreign nations can—the Founder's remedy is to allow government to take property only by laws formally enacted and

---

[146] West, *Ibid.*
[147] West, Ibid.
[148] West, Ibid.
[149] West, Ibid.
[150] West, Ibid.

enforced with appropriate judicial procedures to protect the innocent.[151] Such action, however, is prescribed in the Constitution and clearly expresses the legality of state's action over the citizen.

Today, government's power in the United States has overwhelmingly increased and expanded. Within two centuries of history, the government of the United States has expanded in size and power way beyond its constitutional prerogatives. With the effectuation of the welfare state in the 1930s, and its enlargement in the 1960s; government has intrinsically and exceedingly aggrandized its authority in the economy. The Great Depression was precisely the turning point of that social phenomenon. The economic depression was a boon for government to impose its will on the circumstances of the evolution of the economy. The initial purpose of government intervention in the 1930s, was to

---

[151] West, Ibid.

attenuate the economic recession then to withdraw back to its constitutional purview. But this intervention took a different turn in the economy. For instance, during the 1930s, government imposed the first ever federal minimum wage law, which demonstrated a government bureaucratic infringement into the labor market. Without a federal minimum wage law, business owners had the possibility to stimulate labor demand, labor costs as well as determining prices. The implementation of a federal minimum wage made it impossible for business owners to henceforth fully control labor cost. They had to act according to the guidelines provided by the federal government. additionally, the effectuation of the federal minimum wage law compelled state governments to implement that law in their respective states. States like Texas, Virginia, or Mississippi, which do not have a state minimum wage, are nevertheless compelled to have a minimum wage law. Since federal law overrides state law, these states that do not have a state minimum wage do use the federal minimum wage to determine labor cost and labor demand. Another example is the creation of social security through the Social Security Act; still in the 1930s; which enabled government to collect taxes from the individual's paycheck in order to financially support senior citizens during their retirement. The implementation of this law [Social Security Act] was decisive because it allowed the transition of government authority to move from a temporary state to a permanent one in the economy.

The consolidation of permanent government intervention in the economy was effectuated in the 1960s with the creation of many social welfare programs such as Food Stamps, Affirmative Action laws, Medicare and Medicaid; have empowered government to be unlimited, powerful and exponentially coercive. As of today, the United States, is now a mixed economy like other liberal democracies of the Western Hemisphere. Laissez-faire capitalism is not as prevailing and strong as it used to be. Too many regulations and licenses imposed by government make it even harder for individuals to start a business or to pursue other economic ventures. If the level of income inequality is much higher today than eighty years ago; it is, of course, because of the compulsory redistribution of wealth enforced by government. Indeed, those who receive government-benefits from social programs do become economically emancipated because they have become dependent of these government programs. They receive an income that they have not work to earn it. It is a humongous disincentive that maintain those who benefits from these programs as laggards. They have no motivation to produce. At the same time, the government ensures that the recipients of means-tested benefits continue to believe that it is their savior and benefactor. Limited government allows a better redistribution of wealth when it leaves the market to be the principal factor of that redistribution.

Capitalism is a rewarding economic system. Anyone who substantially produces to the economy; is rewarded for the investment of his production. He makes money and creates wealth from the production of his work. That is the most ethical way to redistribute the wealth. Not by government compulsory taxation.

146

Chapter 9

CAPITALISM
AND
SOCIAL JUSTICE

Social justice is a chief element of an egalitarian society. Not of a capitalistic society. To my understanding, the concept of justice in a capitalist society is more or less summarized as a fair economic justice where everyone has the opportunity and ability to use their skills in the market and produce whatever they can produce. In my understanding, which means from a capitalist mindset, the concept of social justice is the social concept in which any individual has the ability to produce and to enjoy the profit of what he has produced. Speaking of individuals in this context of justice, I refer to individuals who are mentally capacitated to make rational decisions; who are socially responsible; and who are not a source of harm for themselves and to others. It refers to men and women who are free citizens living in a civilized society regardless of their socioeconomic situation. This approach to social justice that I am arguing for does not apply to children because they live under the dependency of their parents, so they cannot and are not able to be financially and socially responsible; nor to individuals with mental disabilities since they are mentally incapacitated to rationally decide for what is good or bad for themselves. It does not mean that they do not deserve justice, or whatsoever; it simply means that they are not involved in this specific subject because they do not control their psychological and socioeconomic condition. This topic chiefly concerns individuals who are mentally fit, and able to be mature enough to rationally decide for themselves. So, for example, an eighteen-year-old individual with no mental disability and unemployed; does fit in my conception of justice. My conception of social justice indicates that justice is served to those who bring value to societal betterment.

Notwithstanding, John Rawls; one of the greatest American political philosophers of all time; who published *A Theory of Justice* in 1971; had a very different approach to the concept of justice than mine. As a matter of fact, Rawls believed that the administration of justice shall be fair to every individual regardless of their socioeconomic condition, whether they are rich or poor. His theory of justice principally envisioned a much more egalitarian society in which individuals would be equal in outcomes; which means that the allocation of social and material goods would be fairly and adequately distributed among people regardless of their socioeconomic condition, by a central authority. A vision of justice that I am vehemently opposed to. Rawls' theory of justice focuses on two principles. One the one hand, the principle of Equal Liberty and on the other hand; the principle of Difference Principle which encapsulates the theory of distributive justice. The Equal Liberty principle argues that each person has an equal right to the most extensive liberties compatible with similar liberties for all.[152] The Difference Principle emphasizes on the premise that social and economic inequalities should be arranged so that they are both to the greatest benefit of the least advantaged persons, and attached to offices and positions open to all under conditions of equality of opportunity.[153] The Equal Liberty principle appeals to an egalitarian approach to liberty since it distributes extensive liberties equally to all persons.[154] Furthermore, it is also an egalitarian model of justice since it distributes opportunities

---

[152] Garrett, Jan. *John Rawls on Justice*, 2011, https://people.wku.edu/jan.garrett/ethics/johnrawl.htm
[153] Garrett, *Ibid.*
[154] Garrett, *Ibid.*

to be considered for offices and positions in an equal manner.[155] The Difference Principle mainly concentrates on the equality of material goods and services. As a practical matter, it stipulates that the wealth of an economy is not a fixed amount from one period to the next, but can be influenced by many factors relevant to economic growth—these include, for example, technological advancement or changes in policy that affect how much people are able to produce with their labor and resources.[156] Since the only material inequalities the Difference Principle permits are those that raise the level of the least advantaged in society, it materially collapses to a form of strict equality under empirical conditions where differences in income have no effect on the work incentive of people.[157] These two principles of

---

[155] Garrett, *Ibid.*

[156] Editors, "Distributive Justice", *Stanford Encyclopedia of Philosophy,* First Published in September 1996, Revised in September 26, (2017), https://plato.stanford.edu/entries/justice-distributive/#EopPri

[157] Editors, *Ibid.*

Rawls; the Equal Liberty principle and the Difference Principle; are undeniably noble objectives. But how these two principles would be applied? Government is the only entity that can solidly carry out and apply these principles that Rawls has advocated for. It tacitly suggests that the effectuation of income equality and the equality of allocation of resources; require government coercion, and a reduction of individual liberties. Freedom and equality cannot fundamentally coexist because if individuals are free; free to pursue their economic self-interests, free to live their lives are they see fit; then they are not and cannot be equal because their incentives are different. If, however, individuals are equal; equal in material and social outcomes; they are not and cannot be free because they are compelled to abide by a set of redistributive rules enforced by government whereupon equality is defined. It also implies that if individuals are equal in material goods; neither of them can pursue their own self-interests because government is the one that dictates which material goods each individual shall possess or acquire. Egalitarianism; in seeking ultimate equality, delivers injustice, economic disparity and suffering; because tyranny is inevitable in order to assure equality of outcome. For example, when the Soviet Union became a superpower, 98 percent of Soviets were equal in their misery because the Soviet government was in control of the redistribution of wealth and resources. So, the 2 percent; which were the individuals working for the Soviet government were the wealthiest. Such example reflects how unequal the Soviet Union was as an egalitarian society. It also demonstrates how unequal egalitarianism is in its nature.

My concept of social justice is entirely different and diametrically antagonistic than that of Mr. Rawls, with all due respect to his work. Social justice in a capitalist society is foremost merit-based. It is merit-based because human beings by nature are unequal. Human beings are naturally and fundamentally unequal because each single one of us is different in behavior, skills, abilities, and talents. Muhammad Ali and Michael Jackson, for example; although are both individuals; they are not equal because they both have a different set of skills in which each of them has exceled. Muhammad Ali was known worldwide for his boxing skills. He won several boxing championships which enabled him to demonstrate his skills as a boxer. Michael Jackson, on the other hand, was also known worldwide for his singing and dancing abilities. He won several awards which confirmed his greatness as a singer and dancer in a special musical genre. Michael Jackson did not have the physical strength of Muhammad Ali and Muhammad Ali did not have the musical talent of Michael Jackson. But they both contributed to the improvement of their respective endeavor and that of society as a whole by bringing people together and having a good time during their respective performances. Muhammad Ali and

Michael Jackson demonstrated to people that anyone can achieve their purpose within the endeavor they pursue. They made boxing, and music attainable careers for individuals who had a passion for these two forms of entertainment.

Justice in capitalism rewards those who contribute to societal advancement. Justice in a capitalist society does not emphasize on equality of outcome because equality is subordinated to productivity to maximize the common good of the organizational entity.[158] It implies that, since human nature is inherent with innate but unequal potentialities among individual; the allocation of goods is distributed according to the productivity of those who stimulate the creation of wealth and capital. Those who produce more get a logically higher income. Capitalism recognizes the equality of opportunity unlike that of outcome. Equality of opportunity advocates that individuals are equal

---

[158] Young, William H., "Social Justice and Capitalism", *National Association of Scholars,* (2013), https://www.nas.org/articles/social_justice_and_capitalism. Article. Web.

on the premise that they have the same opportunity to change their own lives, to take responsibility for themselves, to utilize their skills in an endeavor to produce something valuable and useful. Equality of opportunity; or inequality of outcome; is determined by diversity of learned capabilities and legal equality.[159]

The quintessential element of capitalistic justice is grounded in the Hierarchy of Competence. It is a procedural system by which an individual learns a new skill and through the stages of the process, he becomes better and competent at that skill than when he commenced. Every endeavor has a Hierarchy of Competence. That is why no single individual on earth becomes the best or the greatest in his craft overnight. To become the best requires the maximization of skills and the perpetual update of these skills. Those who maximize their skills are rewarded at the equitable value of their performance. The

---

[159] Young, *Ibid.*

Hierarchy of Competence is significant in that respect because it highlights how an individual becomes competent as he is developing new skills. The process of becoming better at new skills is relatively predictable, and can be broken down into different stages of learning.[160] Once an individual comprehends how this process works, he begins to understand why the beginning of any endeavor is always hard at first, then he is able to identity the position in the learning process.[161] There are chiefly four stages that encapsulate the concept of the Hierarchy of Competence. The first stage is the Unconscious Incompetence. This stage substantiates the commencement of the learning of the new skill. This stage is characterized by the fact that an individual is not cognitive at first of the new skill he has to learn. He is not entirely aware of what the new skill

---

[160] Editors, "The Stages of Learning: How You Slowly Become More Competent at New Skills", *Effectiviology*, https://effectiviology.com/the-stages-of-learning-how-you-slowly-become-more-competent-at-new-skills/
[161] Editors, *Ibid.*

entails, and he is not exactly sure of what his goals should be.[162] The second stage of the Hierarchy of Competence is the Conscious Incompetence. This stage is an intermediate stage of the process.[163] At this stage, the individual begins to familiarize himself with the knowledge of the skill he is developing. Although this stage is still at an archaic and raw level, the individual is now able to recognize and discern certain patterns of the skill which establishes the routine of the process. Moreover, the individual is more cognizant of the mistakes he may make while he is learning the procedure. The third stage of the Hierarchy of Competence is the Conscious Competence. It is the most substantive part of the process because it is the transitional stage in which the individual achieves a level of proficiency. At this stage, the individual is proficient in the procedure and mechanism of the skill that he continues to develop. His familiarity

---

[162] Editors, *Ibid.*
[163] Editors, *Ibid.*

with the knowledge of the skill is fundamentally entrenched, which determines that the learner has indeed the basic knowledge which enables him to hold that proficiency. The fourth and last stage of the Hierarchy of Competence is the Unconscious Competence. This stage is the mastery stage.[164] It is the stage wherein the individual's knowledge of the skill is highly proficient. At this stage, the speed and accuracy of execution of the individual while using the skill is highly procedural, structured, and mechanic. The individual becomes unconsciously competent in the performance of the skill he has developed because he repeatedly performs the same skill all day long within a long-time span. It becomes like a machinery movement. This stage also represents the zenith of the skill he has developed, which is its maximization. He is then an expert at what he does best.

---

[164] Editors, *Ibid.*

Capitalistic distributive justice does not attempt to reward the least disadvantaged or the least fortunate in the allocation of goods; but it rewards under the principle of merit-based. The individual harvest what he has sown. It suggests that it advocates for the Hierarchy of Competence as the basis to determine the value of an individual, and his contribution to the betterment and the enhancement of society. As Ayn Rand has advocated throughout her philosophical career, man in itself is his end and not a means to serve others, so happiness is his ultimate end and reason is the tool by which he uses his knowledge to make his decision. Therefore, the individual is the sole responsible for his own justice, he is the sole responsible for what he produces. Capitalism enables individuals to pursue their incentives freely and without government intervention. Because force is initiated when the individual is compelled to abide by regulations that violate his liberty. Justice under a capitalist system rewards reason, determination, ambition, dedication, discipline and commitment. People who are today rich did not fall from the sky, they became rich because they create, they innovate, and they expand on what they create. Amazon CEO, Jeff Bezos is a perfect example. He started his company very small, then expanded Amazon beyond the imagination of mankind. It is subsequently not surprising that he is currently the richest man in the world. He has shaped the way human beings we able to have access to goods and services without leaving their couch.

CONCLUSION

Capitalism is regrettably the most resented economic system. It is resented for the wrong reasons. Today, many people believe that it is the system that enforces stratification, economic disparities and income inequality. This is the belief that the younger generations are growing with. Yet capitalism is that very economic system that saved lives and improved the living conditions of billions of people. Many former socialist countries such as Estonia, Latvia, Czech Republic, Slovakia, Romania, Bulgaria, Moldova, and the whole Eastern Europe, were all less prosperous than Western Europe as well as the United States because socialism, the collectivization of the means of production, and the mismanagement of resources, have impoverished these nations. The fall of the Berlin Wall, the dissolution of the Soviet Union, and the rejection of socialism have elevated former socialist countries to better living standards. Even China today, whether socialist believers refuse to admit, is no longer a socialist or communist economy. China is a market economy with an authoritarian political regime. The Communist Party of China is a one-party that has confiscated political liberalism but has allowed economic liberalism to its people. Venezuela is today paying the price of the curse of socialism. Social democracies like Scandinavian countries are also market economies with a strong welfare state. But they are still a market economy.

Without a system in which individuals can voluntarily exchange what they own, human capital cannot expand, knowledge cannot be processed, resources cannot be used for production, production cannot create capital, and without capital, there is no wealth to be generated. Capitalism allows this whole process to happen because its essence depends on the knowledge of those who use their skills to innovate new ventures on the market. The power of a free-market economy is determined by knowledge, whether it is intellectual knowledge or practical knowledge. By intellectual knowledge, we suggest knowledge that is acquired from educational achievement such as medical, legal, historical, mathematical, literary or scientific knowledge; and by practical knowledge, we imply knowledge that is acquired by someone who learns the task of the job in which he performs or through apprenticeship. The knowledge of business for instance, is not a knowledge that an individual necessarily obtains in school. Instead, it is a knowledge that is acquired through work, life experience and apprenticeship. Steve Jobs, for example, was a college dropout, who never majored in any specific subject. He did not acquire his knowledge of business through academic achievement but through work and real-life experiences. These two forms of knowledge [intellectual and practical] significantly impact the way economic activities are conveyed. It indicates that knowledge is the decisive factor that, not only determines the value of prices, but it also enables the prediction of economic calculations regarding production. The reason why socialist societies could not prosper is simply because central planners lack the knowledge required to determine the conditions of production such as price, scarcity, and exchange rates. As Ludwig von Mises explained in his book entitled *Socialism* (1922); an economic system such as socialism cannot prevail nor sustain because the economic calculations to determine the production of an economy do not exist in the socialist state. Bureaucrats cannot exchange the materials that the government uses to produce goods and services because these materials have no price to determine their value. Since these materials are state-owned, they have no value. They are used until they become rotten then useless and cannot be unexchanged. Central planners do not understand the utility of price. They do not comprehend that prices are the signals that ensconced the utility and the sustainability of a given product or service. Without prices, materials could not be exchanged.

Socialism confiscates knowledge while capitalism uses it to generate economic incentives. Economic incentives can only take place if those who have the ability to create capital are free to do so. Individuals with economic power, which means private investors, and business owners understand the necessity of prices. Moreover, they fully grasp the concept of human capital. Human capital is what enhances production. When individuals are free to pursue their self-interest, which means they are free to use their skills, talents, and abilities in whatever venture they believe could deliver great outcomes, the aggregate output of the national production exceeds expectations. When people are free to innovate, the economic growth of a whole society substantially improves because there are no regulations to impede economic decisions. The problem with regulations on businesses is that when the government imposes a form of guideline upon which business owners are compelled to follow, it reduces incentives as well as the expansion of human capital. A business either flourishes or perishes based on the output it produces. A business perishes, of course, due to mismanagement, but also due to a lack of substantial human capital. If a business is short in human capital because state regulations prevent the business owner to hire whoever he wants at whatever wage he wants, then that business will not be able to produce more than it was expected. If there was no regulations nor licenses on how a private business should be managed, then the business owner is free to hire whoever, he believes, would fit the needs of the business to thrive. That is why state intervention in the private sector has never benefited those who have the means to stimulate it. State intervention is an attempt to exert a form of authority over price control. As it was expounded in the previous paragraph, if the state is in charge of prices, the materials or products used in that industry being controlled by state regulation could not be exchanged for renovation.

Whether we love capitalism, or hate it; we cannot, nonetheless, deny the fact that capitalism improves the living standard of any given society that uses it as its economic system. We have all witnessed how the living standard in Eastern Europe has substantially incremented since the 1990s. Why? Because Eastern Europeans became free. Free to innovate, and free to undertake. Foreign investments poured into these countries, which created more jobs, and more economic opportunities. The living standard of Eastern European rose because many of them migrated from lower social classes to higher social classes. Capitalism is the fastest way to create wealth because individuals are free to produce. It is important to understand that physical wealth is something that has to be produced otherwise it will never take form. Only skills, talents, and abilities open up the gate to economic prosperity. So, to say that the "rich get richer and the poor get poorer" is a false and misleading premise implanted in the consciousness of the average man by the intelligentsia, the media, and politicians who want to give to the state more control and authority over decision-making. The case of Eastern Europe is a perfect evidence to demonstrate that capitalism makes the poor richer and the rich richer. Everyone wins within a capitalist society. Individuals will never be equal in terms of income, but each member of a capitalist society has the opportunity to lift himself up from one social class to another. The most important to for economic growth to continue to thrive and for the poor to become self-sufficient.

REFERENCES

Edtiors, "Towards the End of Poverty," *The Economist*.(2013). https://www.economist.com/leaders/2013/06/01/towards-the-end-of-poverty. Article. Web.

Amadeo, Kimberly, "Capitalism, Its Characteristics, with Pros and Cons", *The Balance*, Economic Models, Economic Theory, December 29, 2018, https://www.thebalance.com/capitalism-characteristics-examples-pros-cons-3305588. Article. Web.

Amadeo, Ibid.

Amadeo, Ibid.

Amadeo, Ibid.

Amadeo, Ibid.

Amadeo. Ibid.

"Genesis, Chapter 3, Versed 19," The Old Testament, *The Holy Bible.*

Editors of Encyclopedia Britannica, "Division of Labour", *Encyclopedia Britannica,* https://www.britannica.com/topic/division-of-labour. Article History.

Munger, Michael, "Division of Labor", *The Library of Economics and Liberty,* https://www.econlib.org/library/Enc/Divisionof Labor.html. Article. Web.

Munger, Ibid.

Munger, Ibid.

Bruce Lee Quote.

"Division of Labor (Adam Smith)", *General Principles of Management,* https://ozgurzan.com/management/managemen t-theories/adam-smith/. Article. Web.

Pratap, Abhijeet, "Division of Labor: Adam Smith", *Checknotes,* October 1st, 2016, updated in September 28, 2018. https://www.cheshnotes.com/2016/10/division-labor-adam-smith/. Article. Web.

Pratap, Ibid.

Pratap, Ibid.

Reyes, Raul, "An Inquiry Into The Division of Labor" (2013). *University Honors Theses. Paper 27.* https://pdxscholar.library.pdx.edu/cgi/viewcont ent.cgi?article=1024&context=honorstheses

Reyes, Ibid.

Simmons, Ann, "African immigrants are more educated than most—including people born in U.S." *Los Angeles Times.* January 12, 2018. https://www.latimes.com/world/africa/la-fg-global-african-immigrants-explainer-20180112-story.html. Article. Web.

Langone, Alix, "Oprah Winfrey Is Worth Nearly $3 Billion. Here's How She Made Her Money". Time, March 9, 2018, http://time.com/money/5092809/oprah-winfrey-net-worth-billionaire/. Article. Web.

Langone, Ibid.

Langone, Ibid.

Langone, Ibid.

Langone, Ibid.

174

Langone, Ibid.

Langone, Ibid.

Langone, Ibid.

Langone, Ibid.

Shull, Ed, "How Arnold Became Rich", Filthy Lucre, August 8, 2018. https://filthylucre.com/how-arnold-schwarzenegger-became-rich/. Article. Web.

Kenton, Will, "Entrepreneur", Investopedia, March, 20, 2018, Article.

Kenton, Ibid.

Kenton, Ibid.

Shukla, Amitabh, "The Importance of Innovation in Entrepreneurship", *Paggu,* 2017, https://www.paggu.com/entrepreneurship/the-importance-of-innovation-in-entrepreneurship/. Article. Web.

"Concepts and Characteristic of Entrepreneurship"*Entrepreneurship Development,* https://www.toppr.com/guides/business-studies/entrepreneurship-development/concepts-and-characteristics-of-entrepreneurship/. Article. Web.

Ibid.

Ibid.

Ibid.

McCormick, Kristen, "Why Is It Important for Companies To Have Competitors?" *Thrive Hive*, 2016, https://thrivehive.com/why-it-important-companies-have-competitors/. Article. Web.

McCormick, Ibid.

McCormick, Ibid.

Economic System: Capitalism, Communism, and Socialism, https://thismatter.com/economics/economic-systems.htm.

Ibid.

Ibid.

"1. Self-Ownership", Libertarianism, (2002), substantive revision in 2018. *Stanford Encyclopedia of Philosophy*, https://plato.stanford.edu/entries/libertarianism/#SelOwn.

Ibid.

Ibid.

Ibid.

Dr. Shawn Ritenour, "Three reasons Private Property Is Essential for Human Flourishing", The Institute For Faith, Work & Economics, (2014), https://tifwe.org/private-property-and-human-flourishing/. Article. Web.

Ritenour, Ibid.

Ritenour, Ibid.

Ritenour, Ibid.

Ritenour, Ibid.

Ritenour, Ibid.

Ritenour, Ibid.

Ritenour, Ibid.

Ritenour, Ibid.

Ritenour, Ibid.

Ritenour, Ibid.

Ritenour, Ibid.

Horwitz, Steven, "On Human Action: We owe a debt to Ludwig von Mises", *Foundation for Economic Education*, (2012), https://fee.org/articles/on-human-action/. Article. Web.

Horwitz, Ibid.

Horwitz, Ibid.

Horwitz, Ibid.

Horwitz, Ibid.

Horwitz, Ibid.

Brancaglione, Marcus, "Free Market, Free Will, Self-Regulation", Medium Co, (2015), https://medium.com/@mbrancaglione/free-market-free-will-self-regulation-c6a1396bb534. Article. Web.

Kenton, Will, "Chicago School, "Investopedia, (2018), https://www.investopedia.com/terms/c/chicago_school.asp.

Kenton, Ibid.

McCurray, John, "Economist Milton Friedman Championed Free Markets and Individualism", *Investor's Business Daily*, (2016), https://www.investors.com/news/management/leaders-and-success/economist-milton-friedman-championed-free-markets-and-individualism/. Article. Web.

McCurray, Ibid.

Kenton, Will, "Chicago School" Investopedia, (2018), https://www.investopedia.com/terms/c/chicago_school.asp.

Kenton, Ibid.

"Chicago School vs. Austrian School: Battle of the Free-marketeers", *The Economic Review*, September 24, 2011, https://theeconomicreview.wordpress.com/2011/09/24/chicago-school-vs-austrian-school-battle-of-the-free-marketeers/. Article. Web.

Ibid.

Ibid.

Ibid.

Ibid.

Ibid.

Ibid.

Ibid.

Hülsmann, Jörg Guido, "Monetary Policy and the Free Market", Mises Daily Articles, *The Mises Institute,* (2003), https://mises.org/library/monetary-policy-and-free-market. Article. Web.

Hülsmann, Ibid.

Hülsmann, Ibid.

Hülsmann, Ibid.

Hülsmann, Ibid.

Hülsmann, Ibid.

Hülsmann, Ibid.

Woolsey, Bill, "Free Market Economists and Monetary Policy", *Monetary Freedom,* (2010). http://monetaryfreedom-billwoolsey.blogspot.com/2010/11/bryan-caplan-asks-why-free-market.html. Article. Web.

Woolsey, Ibid.

Woolsey, Ibid.

Chen, James, "Monetary Policy, *Investopedia*, (2018).
https://www.investopedia.com/terms/m/monetarypolicy.asp.

Chen, Ibid.

Chen, Ibid.

Chen, Ibid.

Amadeo, Kimberly, "Types of Inflation: The Four Most Critical Plus Nine More: Including Asset, Wage, and Core Inflation", The Balance, December 22, 2018, https://www.thebalance.com/types-of-inflation-4-different-types-plus-more-3306109. Article. Web.

Amadeo, Ibid.

Amadeo, Ibid.

Amadeo, Ibid.

Amadeo, Ibid.

Amadeo, Ibid.

Amadeo, Ibid.

Amadeo, Ibid.

Amadeo, Ibid.

Amadeo, Ibid.

Amadeo, Ibid.

Weil, David, "Fiscal Policy", *The Library of Economics and Liberty,* 2018, https://www.econlib.org/library/Enc/FiscalPolicy.html. Article.

Weil, Ibid.

Weil, Ibid.

Weil, Ibid.

Weil, Ibid.

Weil, Ibid.

Weil, Ibid.

Quote By Ayn Rand

"Individual Rights", *Business Dictionary.* http://www.businessdictionary.com/definition/individual-rights.html.

"Introduction: Aristotle's Definition of Happiness", Aristotle, The pursuit of Happiness-Bringing the Science of Happiness To Life, https://www.pursuit-of-happiness.org/history-of-happiness/aristotle/.

Salsman, Richard M. "Individual Rights and The Essential Nature of Capitalism", *Capitalism Magazine*, December 22, 1999, https://www.capitalismmagazine.com/1999/12/individual-rights-and-the-essential-nature-of-capitalism/. Article. Web.

Salsman, Ibid.

Salsman, Ibid.

Salsman, Ibid.

Salsman, Ibid.

Rand, Ayn, Capitalism: The Unknown Ideal, 1966, *Ayn Rand Institute*, https://www.aynrand.org/novels/capitalism-the-unknown-ideal.

Rand, Ayn, "Man's Rights", The Virtue of Selfishness,(1963), https://ari.aynrand.org/issues/government-and-business/individual-rights. Essay.

Rand, Ibid.

Rand, Ibid.

Rand, Ibid.

Younkins, Edward, "Perspective on Capitalism and Freedom: The Proper Role of The State is Limited", *Foundation For Economic Education*, 1996, https://fee.org/articles/perspectives-on-capitalism-and-freedom/.

Younkins, Ibid.

Younkins, Ibid.

Younkins, Ibid.

Younkins, Ibid.

Younkins, Ibid.

"DenmarkPopulation"
http://www.worldometers.info/world-population/denmark-population/

"NorwayPopulation"
http://www.worldometers.info/world-population/norway-population/

"SwedenPopulation"
http://www.worldometers.info/world-population/sweden-population/

184

"FinlandPopulation"
http://www.worldometers.info/world-population/finland-population/

"IcelandPopulation"
http://www.worldometers.info/world-population/iceland-population/

Wolverton, Joe, "James Madison and Limited Government", *New American-That Freedom Shall Not Perish,* (2010), https://www.thenewamerican.com/culture/history/item/4781-james-madison-and-limited-government. Article. Web.

Wolverton, Ibid.

Wolverton, Ibid.

Wolverton, Ibid.

Wolverton, Ibid.

Wolverton, Ibid.

Wolverton, Ibid.

West, Thomas, "The Economic Principles of America's Founders: Property Rights, Free Markets, and Sound Money", *The Heritage Foundation,* (2010), https://www.heritage.org/political-process/report/the-economic-principles-americas-founders-property-rights-free-markets-and. Article. Web.

West, Ibid.

West, Ibid.

West, Ibid.

West, Ibid.

West, Ibid.

West, Ibid.

West, Ibid.

West, Ibid.

Garrett, Jan. John Rawls on Justice, 2011, https://people.wku.edu/jan.garrett/ethics/johnrawl.htm

Garrett, Ibid.

Garrett, Ibid.

Garrett, Ibid.

Editors, "Distributive Justice", *Stanford Encyclopedia of Philosophy*, First Published in September 1996, Revised in September 26, (2017), https://plato.stanford.edu/entries/justice-distributive/#EopPri

Editors, Ibid.

Young, William H., "Social Justice and Capitalism", *National Association of Scholars*, (2013), https://www.nas.org/articles/social_justice_and_capitalism. Article. Web.

Young, Ibid.

Editors, "The Stages of Learning: How You Slowly Become More Competent at New Skills",*Effectiviology*, https://effectiviology.com/the-stages-of-learning-how-you-slowly-become-more-competent-at-new-skills/
Editors, Ibid.

Editors, Ibid.

Editors, Ibid.

Editors, Ibid.

CPSIA information can be obtained
at www.ICGtesting.com
Printed in the USA
FSHW010501011121
85880FS